Freshwater Fish *of* North America

Field Guide

Dave Bosanko & Dan Johnson

Adventure Publications

Edited by Kate Johnson and Emily Beaumont

Cover and book design by Jonathan Norberg

Illustration credits on page 271.

10 9 8 7 6 5 4 3 2

Freshwater Fish of North America Field Guide

Published by Adventure Publications
An imprint of AdventureKEEN
310 Garfield Street South
Cambridge, Minnesota 55008
(800) 678-7006
adventurepublications.net

Printed in China
Library of Congress Control Number: 2025948370
ISBN 978-1-64755-606-8 (pbk.); 978-1-64755-607-5 (ebook)

TABLE OF CONTENTS

Sunfish Family

Temperate Bass Family

ABOUT THIS BOOK

This quick, convenient, and easy-to-use field guide will help you identify more than 120 of the most common species of freshwater fish found in North America. It includes all of the major sport fish, as well as representatives from every common fish family found on the continent. Each species account includes illustrations and written descriptions that cover everything from habitat and range to similar-looking species. For the game species, we even provide tips to help you catch more fish.

HOW TO USE THIS BOOK

The fish are organized by family, such as catfish (Ictaluridae) and sunfish (Centrarchidae). Each family is then listed in alphabetical order (with a few exceptions). Within these families, individual species are arranged alphabetically in their appropriate groups. For example, members of the sunfish family are divided into black bass, crappie, and true sunfish groups. For a detailed list of fish families and individual species, turn to the table of contents (page 3). The index (page 267) provides a reference guide to fish by common name (such as mooneye) and other common terms for the species.

Fish Identification

Determining a fish's body shape is the first step to identifying it. Each fish family usually exhibits one or sometimes two basic outlines. Catfish have long, stout bodies with flattened heads; barbels, or "whiskers," around the mouth; a relatively tall but narrow dorsal fin; and an adipose fin. Sunfish have two forms: the flat, round, platelike outline seen in bluegills and the torpedo, or fusiform, shape of largemouth bass.

In this field guide, you can quickly identify a fish by first matching its general body shape to one of the fish family silhouettes listed in the table of contents. From there, turn to that family's section and use the illustrations and text descriptions to identify your fish. The sample pages (pages 26–27) explain how the information is presented in each two-page species account.

For some species, the illustration will be enough to identify your catch, but it's important to note that your fish may not look exactly like the artwork. Fish frequently change colors. Males that are brightly colored during the spawning season may show muted coloration at other times. Similarly, bass caught in muddy streams show much less pattern than those taken from clear lakes. And all fish lose some of their markings and color when removed from the water.

Most fish are similar in appearance to one or more other species, often within the same family.

For example, the walleye is remarkably similar to the sauger. To accurately identify such look-alikes, check the inset illustrations and accompanying notes below the main illustration, under the "Similar Species" heading.

Throughout this guide, we use basic biological and fisheries-management terms that refer to physical characteristics or conditions of fish and their environment, such as "dorsal fin" or "turbid water." For your convenience, these are listed and defined in the glossary (page 262). Understanding such terminology will help you make sense of reports on state and federal research, fish surveys, lake assessments, management plans, and other important fisheries documents.

FISH ANATOMY

To identify fish, you will need to know a few basic terms that apply to fins and their locations.

Fins are made up of bony structures that support a membrane. There are three kinds of bony structures in fins. **Soft rays** are flexible fin supports that are sometimes branched. **Spines** are stiff, often sharp supports that are not jointed. **Hard rays** are stiff, pointed, barbed structures that can be raised or lowered. Catfish are famous for their hard rays, which are mistakenly called spines. Sunfish have soft rays associated with spines to form a dorsal fin.

Fins are named by their position on the fish. The **dorsal fin** is on the top along the midline. A few fish have another fin on their back called an **adipose fin.** This is a small, fleshy protuberance located between the dorsal fin and the tail and is distinctive of trout and catfish.

On each side of the fish near the gills are the **pectoral fins.** The **anal fin** is located along the midline on the fish's bottom, or ventral, side. There is also a paired set of fins on the bottom of the fish called the **pelvic fins.** Pelvic fins can be in the **thoracic position** just below the pectoral fins or farther back on the stomach in the **abdominal position.** The tail is known as the **caudal fin.**

Eyes—In general, fish have good eyesight. They can see color, but the light level they require to see well varies by species. For example, walleyes see well and are active in low light, which is why anglers often target them in overcast or choppy conditions. On the other hand, bluegills have excellent daytime vision but see poorly at night, making them vulnerable to predation. Catfish have poor vision both night and day.

Nostrils—Two nostrils, or nares, are used to detect odors in the water. Eels and catfish have a particularly well developed sense of smell.

Mouth—The shape of the mouth is a clue to what the fish eats. The larger the food it consumes, the larger the mouth.

Teeth—Not all fish have teeth, but those that do use them to feed. Walleyes, northern pike, and muskies have sharp canine teeth for grabbing and holding prey. Minnows have teeth located in the throat that are used for grinding. Catfish have cardiform teeth, which feel like a rough patch in the front of the mouth. Bass have tiny patches of teeth on the roof of their mouth; these are called vomerine teeth.

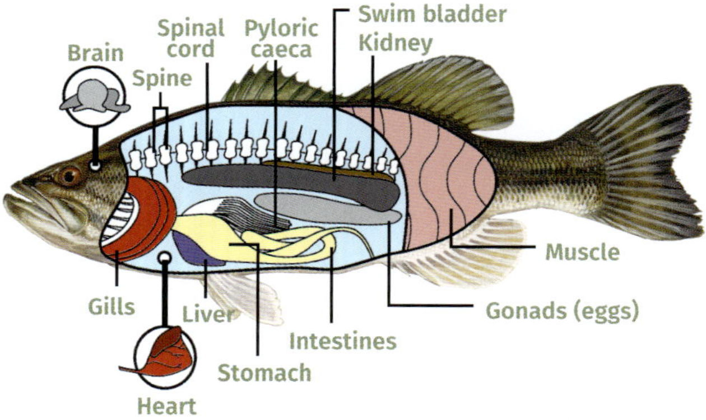

Swim Bladder—Almost all fish have a swim bladder, which is a balloon-like organ that helps regulate buoyancy.

Lateral Line—This sensory organ helps the fish detect movement in the water (to help avoid predators or capture prey), as well as currents and pressure changes. It consists of fluid-filled sacs, with hairlike sensors, that are open to the water through a row of pores in the skin along each side. These pores create a visible line down the middle of the fish's side.

FISH NAMES

Many fish have a number of common names, and they often vary geographically. Consider the largemouth bass; depending on where you are, it may be called a black bass, a green bass, a slough bass, a green trout, or even a bucket mouth.

Because common names vary and can even change for different sizes of the same species, biologists use scientific names. Each species has only one correct scientific name that can be recognized anywhere, in any language. For example, the walleye is *Sander vitreus* from Minneapolis to Moscow.

Scientific names are made up of Greek or Latin words that often describe the species. There are two parts to a scientific name: the generic name, or genus, which is capitalized (*Sander*), and the specific name, which is not capitalized (*vitreus*). Both are italicized or underlined. A genus represents a closely related group of fish. The walleye and sauger are in the same genus, so they share the generic name *Sander*. But each fish has a different specific name: *vitreus* for walleye, *canadensis* for sauger.

THE FISH OF NORTH AMERICA

Freshwater covers about 7% of the United States—over 3.5 million square miles—and over 9% of Canada. While some of that water isn't suitable for fish, much of it is, leading to an almost unlimited number of habitats.

There are over 1,200 kinds of freshwater fish found in North America. Some are game fish or sport fish—species that people enjoy fishing for—while many others are simply interesting creatures that inhabit our lakes and streams. This book is a broad introduction to some of those species.

Some fish are generalists and can live in much of the warmer water found in the country. For example, bluegills are at home in big rivers, small streams, large reservoirs, and small ponds. Sacramento perch can survive in brackish (salty) water streams near the surf line. Rainbow trout and mountain whitefish prefer cold, well-oxygenated water and would not do well in the warm, sluggish streams that alligator gar reside in. Each fish species has its preferred habitat where it will thrive and be most at home. Learning about the habitat preferences of a target species is a great way to catch more fish.

Some fish can be found in most states; others have greatly restricted ranges. The desert pupfish is found only in the warm, salty pools of the desert Southwest. Some fish are naturally widely distributed by being part of large river systems like the Mississippi and the Columbia. Other fish have needed a little help to expand their range. Many of our common game fish have been stocked to provide fishing opportunities. Largemouth bass and rainbow trout have been introduced to most of the United States and around the world. The fathead minnow hitched a ride in bait pails to expand its range. Some species that have been introduced, either by accident or on purpose, have become invasive and are detrimental to native fish and habitats.

FISH BIOLOGY

Though fish come in many different shapes, they can be described generally as aquatic vertebrates that have gills throughout their lives (unlike amphibians, which lose their gills as adults) and have limbs in the form of fins (if they have limbs). Most get oxygen from water passing over their gills, but a few can gulp air and use their swim bladder as a primitive lung. Most fish have hard bones, but some primitive varieties that have persisted for millions of years, such as sharks and sturgeons, have cartilage instead. Scales cover most fish, but some, like catfish, are protected only by skin.

FISH DIVERSITY

Worldwide, there are many different kinds of fish. Of all the vertebrates on Earth, half are fish. There about 28,000 different species, and they have adapted to survive in a range of aquatic environments. Some live in salt water, some live in freshwater, and others prefer a mix (known as brackish water). Some fish live exclusively in salt water or freshwater, and some live in salt water and spawn in freshwater.

Globally, perhaps 12,000 species live in freshwater. About 1,200 freshwater species swim in the lakes and rivers of the United States. A hundred or so species found in the US are not native; these have been introduced in the last 200 years and are now well established. Sadly, about 40 species of our native fish have gone extinct, and a handful more will do so soon.

ADAPTATIONS AND REPRODUCTION

Evolutionary adaptions to different habitats have led to the wide variety of appearances and behaviors we see in fish today. Pikes are long and sleek, built for speed, while sunfish are flat, enabling them to pass in between the weeds. Mooneyes have big eyes for seeing in silty water, and catfish have barbels to help them find food in the dark. Some fish are specialists, meaning they are restricted to only one habitat or food source, while others are generalists, able to tolerate a large range of water conditions and a more varied diet. For example, some members of the pupfish family are specialists; they have adapted to live in hot, salty desert pools and have a very restricted range. A generalist like the black buffalo has adapted to live in large rivers, and its range includes much of the central US.

There are about as many different behaviors involved in fish reproduction as there are fish. Most fish reproduce via external fertilization, with the female shedding eggs that are then fertilized by the male. But the mosquitofish has internal fertilization, and the mother gives birth to live young. Sunfish and many other species build nests and may guard the young. Others, like the white bass, broadcast their eggs to develop on their own. Most fish spawn close to where they live, but salmon travel many miles up streams to spawn, and the American eel swims across an ocean to lay its eggs. All fish, unlike mammals and birds, lay more eggs as they get larger. For example, in a small lake, a few of the biggest females may be laying most of the eggs.

HOW FISH SWIM

Fish swim by flipping their tail back and forth. The fins are mostly used for turning and keeping the fish oriented vertically as they swim. To travel backward, fish twist the pectoral fins to provide the power, and the tail is used for steering. Fish also have an air sac called a swim bladder that keeps them afloat. Without the swim bladder, fish would sink to the bottom if they weren't actively swimming. Many fish, like bass, have only the ribs and backbone for the muscles to pull against. In carp and pike, free-floating bones are sandwiched between the muscles for added strength.

FISH PERCEPTION

Fish perceive their watery world much differently than we do. They can see color, but what exactly they see and how it is different than our vision is difficult to know. Anatomical differences aside, light passing through water acts differently than light passing through air. Water absorbs the wavelengths that correspond to the color red, so red turns to brown under about 10 feet of water. The underwater world is also much darker, limiting a fish's ability to see detail, so they have adapted ways of feeling and even tasting their environment. Hairlike sensors inside the pores of the lateral line can detect pressure changes and electrical currents. This very sensitive structure detects not only water depth but also the passing of other fish; the electrical receptors can detect minute electrical currents created by other fish as they swim. Fish also sample the water passing through their mouth and over their gills; this allows fish to analyze the world around them.

A BIT ABOUT FISHING

People have been fishing for food since prehistoric times. As the technology of nets, boats, and aquaculture (fish farming) advanced, fish became one of the leading sources of animal protein for humans. While mammals and birds are now larger protein sources, fish remain an important protein source in many places.

Fishing for sport also has a long history. Art from ancient Egypt depicts pharaohs sitting on gilded chairs in boats with fishing poles in their hands. Today, many people around the world enjoy sportfishing, from kids at the creek with stick and line fishing for creek chubs to oceangoing boats participating in billfish tournaments.

GEAR AND EQUIPMENT

Technology has improved the chances for finding fish. Better boats and motors get anglers to fishing spots faster and in more comfort, and cameras and sonar help locate and spot the fish, but knowledge and technique are still required to get fish in the boat.

FISH POPULATIONS IN DECLINE

As many aspects of fishing are changing, so are fish populations. Some fish, like crappie, are mostly self-sustaining and need only a little help from catch limits to remain plentiful. For others, habitat degradation, such as silting of spawning beds, may significantly affect their reproduction and/or development; walleye lakes are a good example of this. Stocking may help keep some of these populations healthy, at least for a time, but overall, fish populations—whether in the ocean or in lakes and streams—are declining.

Anglers are an important part of maintaining healthy fish populations. With more leisure time, better equipment, and better information networks, more of them are on the water, and they are catching more fish. Catch-and-release fishing, restricting the movement of invasive species, and supporting clean water efforts can all help sustain our fish populations and keep fishing a pastime that is available to everyone.

FREQUENTLY ASKED QUESTIONS

What Is a Fish?

Fish are aquatic, typically cold-blooded animals that have backbones, gills, and fins.

Are All Fish Cold-Blooded?

All freshwater fish are cold-blooded. Recently it has been discovered that some members of the saltwater tuna family are warm-blooded. Whales and bottlenose dolphins are also warm-blooded, but they are mammals, not fish.

Do All Fish Have Scales?

No. Most fish have scales that look like those on the common goldfish. A few, such as the gars, have scales that resemble armor plates. Catfish and eels have no scales at all and are covered with a tough skin.

How Do Fish Breathe?

A fish takes in water through its mouth and forces it through its gills, where a system of fine membranes absorbs oxygen from the water and releases carbon dioxide. Gills cannot pump air efficiently over these membranes, which quickly dry out and stick together. If you want a fish to survive, its gills should never be allowed to dry out before returning it to the water.

Can Fish Breathe Air?

Some species can; gar have a modified swim bladder that acts like a lung. Fish that can't breathe air may die when dissolved oxygen in the water falls below critical levels.

How Do Fish Swim?

Fish swim by contracting bands of muscles on alternating sides of the body so the tail is whipped rapidly from side to side. Pectoral and pelvic fins are used mainly for stability and steering when the fish swims or hovers. Sometimes these fins are used during rapid bursts of forward motion or as "legs" to support or move the fish along the bottom. Fish control their depth by inflating or deflating an air sac called the swim bladder.

Do All Fish Look Like Fish?

Most do and are easily recognizable as fish. The eels and lampreys are fish, but they look like snakes. Sculpins look like little goblins with bat wings.

FISH DISEASES

Fish are susceptible to various parasites, infections, and diseases. Some diseases have little effect on fish populations, while others may have a devastating impact. While fish diseases and parasites can't be transmitted to humans, they may render the fish inedible, or at least not appetizing. To prevent the spread of such diseases, take care not to transfer any fish from one body of water to another. You can find information on your local fish diseases and parasites through your state's department of natural resources.

INVASIVE SPECIES

While some introduced species, such as brown trout (introduced from Europe) have great recreational value, many non-native species have caused problems. Helping limit the spread of these nuisance species is everyone's responsibility. Never move fish, water, or vegetation from one lake or stream to another, and always follow your state's recommendations on protecting our water habitats. Details about aquatic invasive species are available at each state's department of natural resources or wildlife management agency.

FUN WITH FISH

There are many ways to enjoy our country's fish, from reading about them in this book to watching them in the wild, keeping an aquarium, or catching one for dinner. And of course, many millions of people enjoy fishing. The sport offers a great chance to enjoy the outdoors with friends and family and, in many cases, bring home a healthy meal of fresh fish.

Proceeds from license sales, along with special taxes on fishing supplies and motorboat fuel, fund the majority of fish management efforts, including surveys, development of special regulations, and stocking programs. The sport also has a huge impact on the country's economy, supporting thousands of jobs in fishing, tourism, and other related industries.

FISH CONSUMPTION ADVISORIES

Fish are often safe to eat, but pollutants are a valid concern. Each state routinely monitors contaminant levels in its waters and issues advisories and recommendations about eating sport fish caught in the wild. For up-to-date consumption guidelines where you're fishing, visit your state's department of natural resources or wildlife management agency.

CATCH-AND-RELEASE FISHING

Selective harvest (keeping some fish to eat and releasing the rest) and total catch-and-release fishing allow anglers to enjoy the sport without overly harming the resource. Catch-and-release is especially important with certain species and sizes of fish and in lakes or rivers where biologists are trying to improve the fishery by protecting adult fish of breeding age. Many lakes now have mandatory slot limits that require anglers to release fish in certain size categories. Check your state's fishing regulations for updates.

Catch-and-release is only truly successful if the fish survives the experience. Here are some helpful tips to reduce the chances of post-release mortality.

- Play and land fish quickly.
- Wet your hands before touching a fish to avoid removing its protective slime coating.
- Handle the fish gently and keep it in the water as much as possible.
- Do not hold the fish by the eyes or gills. Hold it by the lower lip or under the gills to support its belly.
- If a fish is deeply hooked, cut the line so at least an inch hangs outside the mouth. This helps the hook lie flat when the fish takes in food.
- Circle hooks may help reduce the number of deeply hooked fish.
- Avoid fishing in very deep water unless you plan to keep your catch; fish quickly brought up to the surface often suffer damage to their swim bladder, which can be fatal.

FISH MEASUREMENT

Fish length is measured in three ways: standard length, fork length, and total length. The first two are more accurate because tails are often damaged or worn down. Total length is used in slot and overall size limits in most states and is measured by pinching the tail together to make the fish as long as possible.

Tracking fish weights isn't as popular as it once was, but for records and bragging rights, fish weights are often recorded. The following formulas can be used to estimate the weight of popular game fish, though they are only an estimate. Lengths are in inches; weights are in pounds.

Formulas

Bass weight = (length x length x girth) / 1,200
Pike weight = (length x length x length) / 3,500
Sunfish weight = (length x length x length) / 1,200
Trout weight = (length x girth x girth) / 800
Walleye weight = (length x length x length) / 2,700

For example, let's say you catch a 16-inch walleye. Using the formula for walleyes above: 16 (length) x 16 (length) x 16 (length) = 4,096, divided by 2,700 = 1.5. Your walleye would weigh approximately 1.5 pounds.

Most states keep trophy records for common game fish. Many states now have separate records for catch-and-release fish and those taken other than on hook and line (such as via bow). You can summit a fish or check the records through your state's department of natural resources website. The International Game Fish Association keeps very accurate world records for most fish targeted by fishers.

These pages explain how the information is presented for each fish.

SAMPLE FISH ILLUSTRATION

Description: brief summary of physical characteristics to help you identify the fish, such as coloration and markings, body shape, and fin size and placement

Similar Species: other fish that look similar and the pages on which they can be found, along with detailed inset drawings (below) highlighting physical traits such as markings, mouth size or shape, and fin characteristics to help you distinguish this fish from similar species

Largemouth Bass

mouth extends beyond dark orange eye

Smallmouth Bass

mouth does not extend beyond red eye

Common Family Name

Scientific Family Name

COMMON NAME

Scientific Name

Other Names: common terms or nicknames you may hear to describe the species

Habitat: environment where the fish is found (such as streams, rivers, small or large lakes, fast-flowing or still water, in or around vegetation, near shore, in clear water)

Range: geographic distribution across the US

Food: what the fish eats most of the time (such as crustaceans, insects, fish, or plankton)

Reproduction: timing and behavior during the spawning period, season and water temperature, migration information, preferred spawning habitat, type of nest, parental care for eggs or fry

Average Size: the size you will commonly expect to catch across the US; three times this size is a bragging fish but probably not a state record; some small fish are rarely caught, and even if they are, they aren't weighed by anglers; in these cases, no weight is listed

Fishing Tip: a tip to help you catch more fish

Notes: interesting natural history information, such as unique behaviors, remarkable features, sporting and table quality, details on migrations, seasonal patterns, or population trends

Description: brownish-green back and sides with a white belly; long, stout body; rounded tail; continuous dorsal fin; bony plates covering head; large eyespot at the base of the tail on males

Similar Species: burbot (page 50)

Bowfin

no barbel on chin

Burbot

small barbel on chin

Bowfin

one dorsal fin, short anal fin

Burbot

two dorsals, long anal fin

BOWFIN

Amia calva

Other Names: dogfish, grindle or grinnel, mudfish, cypress trout, lake lawyer, beaverfish

Habitat: deep water associated with vegetation in warm-water lakes and rivers; feeds in shallow weedbeds

Range: Mississippi River drainage east through the St. Lawrence River drainage; Gulf slope drainage from Texas to Florida

Food: fish, crayfish

Reproduction: In spring when water exceeds 61° F; male removes vegetation to build a 2-foot-wide nest in sand or gravel; one or more females deposit up to 5,000 eggs in nest; male tenaciously guards the nest and "ball" of young.

Average Size: 12–24 in., 2–5 lb.

Fishing Tip: At night, cast large, active plugs along weedbeds close to deep water.

Notes: A voracious predator, the bowfin prowls shallow weedbeds, preying on anything that moves. Once thought detrimental to game fish populations, it is now considered an asset in controlling rough fish and stunted game fish. An air breather that tolerates low oxygen levels, the bowfin can survive short periods buried in mud. It's not thought of as a good food fish by most people.

Description: black-to-olive-green back; yellowish-green sides; creamy-white-to-yellow belly; light bar at base of tail; barbels around mouth are dark at base; adipose fin; lacks scales; round tail; anal fin with 17–21 rays

Similar Species: brown bullhead (page 32), yellow bullhead (page 34), flathead catfish (page 40), madtom/stonecat (page 42)

Black Bullhead

overbite

Flathead Catfish

underbite

Black Bullhead

free adipose fin

Madtom/ Stonecat

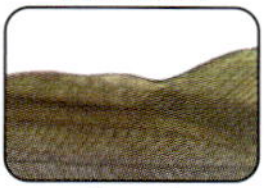

fused adipose fin

Black Bullhead

olive back and sides

Brown Bullhead

mottled back and sides

Yellow Bullhead

yellowish back and sides

BLACK BULLHEAD

Ameiurus melas

Other Names: common bullhead, horned pout

Habitat: shallow, slow-moving streams and backwater lakes and ponds; tolerates extremely turbid conditions

Range: Southern Canada through the Great Lakes and the Mississippi River watershed to the Southwest and into Mexico, introduced west of the Rocky Mountains

Food: a scavenging opportunist; feeds on animal material (dead or alive) and some plant matter

Reproduction: Spawns late April–early June; builds nest in shallow water with a muddy bottom; both sexes guard nest, eggs, and young until they are 1 inch long.

Average Size: 8–10 in., 4–16 oz.

Fishing Tip: In still water, fish the bottom with worms or cut bait.

Notes: The smallest of the four bullhead species found in the US, it is also the most tolerant of silt, pollution, and low oxygen levels. The number of black bullheads has greatly increased since the 1920s. Bullheads get little respect but are tasty and often larger than most of the panfish taken home to eat.

Description: yellowish-brown upper body, with mottling on back and sides; barbels around mouth; adipose fin; scaleless body; rounded tail; well-defined barbs on the pectoral spines: anal fin with 22–23 rays

Similar Species: black bullhead (page 30), yellow bullhead (page 34), flathead catfish (page 40), madtom/stonecat (page 42)

Black Bullhead

overbite

Flathead Catfish

underbite

Black Bullhead

free adipose fin

Madtom/ Stonecat

fused adipose fin

Brown Bullhead

mottled back and sides

Black Bullhead

olive back and sides

Yellow Bullhead

yellowish back and sides

BROWN BULLHEAD

Ameiurus nebulosus

Other Names: marbled or speckled bullhead, red cat

Habitat: warm, weedy lakes and sluggish streams

Range: native east of Rocky Mountains in US and southern Canada; introduced in the West

Food: a scavenging opportunist; feeds mostly on insects, fish, fish eggs, snails, and leeches but will eat plant matter

Reproduction: In early summer, male builds nest in shallow water with good vegetation and a sandy or rocky bottom; both sexes guard the eggs and young.

Average Size: 8–12 in, 8 oz.–2 lb.

Fishing Tip: At night, still-fish on the bottom with worms or cut bait.

Notes: The brown bullhead is most abundant in warm river backwaters, but it also inhabits some cool northern lakes. It has a tendency to inhabit larger, deeper water than other bullheads. It can tolerate very cloudy conditions but prefers clean water with weedy cover and a soft bottom. Adults are very involved in rearing their young, first by agitating the eggs, then by guarding the fry until they grow to about 1 inch long. The young are black and can often be seen swimming in a tight, swarming ball. The meat is red, firm, and very good when pan-fried.

Description: olive head and back; yellowish-green sides; white belly; pale-green or white barbels on lower jaw; adipose fin; scaleless body; rounded tail; anal fin with 24–27 rays

Similar Species: black bullhead (page 30), brown bullhead (page 32), flathead catfish (page 40), madtom/stonecat (page 42)

Yellow Bullhead

overbite

Flathead Catfish

underbite

Yellow Bullhead

free adipose fin

Madtom/ Stonecat

fused adipose fin

Yellow Bullhead

yellowish back and sides

Black Bullhead

olive back and sides

Brown Bullhead

mottled back and sides

YELLOW BULLHEAD

Ameiurus natalis

Other Names: white-whiskered bullhead, yellow cat

Habitat: well-vegetated, warm lakes and sluggish streams

Range: southern Great Lakes through the eastern half of the US to the Gulf and into Mexico; introduced in the West

Food: a scavenging opportunist, feeds on insects, crayfish, snails, small fish, and plant material

Reproduction: In late spring to early summer, males build nests in shallow water with some vegetation and a soft bottom; both sexes guard the eggs and young.

Average Size: 8–10 in., ½–1½ lb.

Fishing Tip: Still-fish the lake bottom with worms or cut bait.

Notes: The yellow bullhead is the bullhead species least tolerant of turbidity. It prefers low-gradient streams but will occupy reasonably clear lakes. Bullheads feed by "taste," locating food by following chemical trails through the water. This ability can be greatly diminished in polluted water, impairing their ability to find food. The yellow bullhead is less likely than other bullhead species to overpopulate a lake and become stunted.

Description: pale-blue back and sides; large fish may be dark bluish gray; no spots or scales; forked tail; anal fin straight on rear edge, with 30–35 rays; adipose fin; long barbels around a small mouth

Similar Species: channel catfish (page 38), flathead catfish (page 40), bullheads (pages 30, 32, and 34)

Blue Catfish

deeply forked tail

Flathead Catfish

squared tail

Bullheads

rounded or slightly notched tail

Blue Catfish

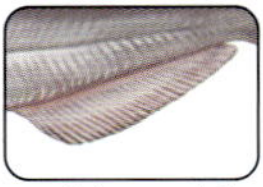

straight anal fin with 30 or more rays

Channel Catfish

curved anal fin with 24–29 rays

BLUE CATFISH

Ictalurus furcatus

Other Names: white, silver, Mississippi, or river cat

Habitat: swift current or deep, flowing pools in large rivers and impoundments; stocked in smaller impoundments for specialized fishing

Range: native to major rivers of Mississippi, Missouri, and Ohio River basins south to northeastern Mexico

Food: small fish; often dead or injured shad

Reproduction: Adults mature at 4–6 years; spawning occurs in sheltered areas at the edge of currents, often in cavities or behind rocks; eggs and fry are guarded by adults.

Average Size: 2–3 ft., 15–25 lb., 40 lb. not uncommon

Fishing Tip: Fish in deep, moving water with a ledge, such as the edge of a shipping channel.

Notes: Blue cats are big fish that inhabit the fast waters of large river systems and their impoundments. Before these rivers were dammed, blue catfish were widespread in the central states but now are very uncommon north of Iowa. Limited stocking has been unsuccessful. Often, smaller ones are mistaken for older channel catfish; be sure to check the mouth and anal fins to be sure what you have caught.

Description: steel-gray-to-silver back and sides; white belly; young fish have black spots on the sides; large fish lack spots and appear dark olive or slate gray; forked tail; adipose fin; long barbels around mouth; anal fin with rounded edge

Similar Species: blue catfish (page 36), flathead catfish (page 40), bullheads (pages 30, 32, and 34)

Channel Catfish

deeply forked tail

Flathead Catfish

squared tail

Bullheads

rounded or slightly notched tail

Channel Catfish

curved anal fin with 24–29 rays

Blue Catfish

straight anal fin with 30 or more rays

CHANNEL CATFISH

Ictalurus punctatus

Other Names: spotted, speckled, or silver catfish

Habitat: prefers clean, fast-moving streams with deep pools; stocked in many lakes; can tolerate turbid waters

Range: native to central drainages of the US; widely introduced in the US and other countries

Food: insects, crustaceans, fish, some plant debris

Reproduction: In early summer, the male builds a nest in a sheltered area, like undercut banks or behind logs; the male guards the eggs and young until the nest is deserted.

Average Size: 12–20 in., 1–4 lb.

Fishing Tip: At night, fish in a riffle at the head of a deep hole, using frogs as bait. During the day, fish brush piles with cut bait.

Notes: Channel catfish are hard fighters and considered fine table fare, though their popularity varies over their range. They are one of the most adaptable catfish and have been introduced to most suitable habitats throughout the US. Channel catfish have highly variable growth rates, with some water consistently producing above average–size fish. They were the first widely farmed food fish in the US and are now common in grocery stores and restaurants.

Description: variable color, usually mottled yellow or brown; cream-to-yellow belly; adipose fin; chin barbels; lacks scales; squared tail; broad and flattened head; pronounced underbite

Similar Species: channel catfish (page 38), bullheads (pages 30, 32, and 34), tadpole madtom (page 42)

Flathead Catfish

squared tail

Channel Catfish

deeply forked tail

Tadpole Madtom

adipose fin fused to tail

Flathead Catfish

underbite

Channel Catfish

overbite

Bullheads

overbite

FLATHEAD CATFISH

Pylodictis olivaris

Other Names: shovelnose, shovelhead; yellow, mud, pied, or Mississippi cat

Habitat: deep pools of large rivers and impoundments

Range: native to Mississippi, Missouri, and Ohio River basins; Gulf Slope drainage from west Florida to Mexico; limited introductions

Food: fish, crayfish

Reproduction: Spawns when water temperature reaches 65° F–80° F; male builds and defends nest in hollow logs, undercut banks, or other sheltered areas; large females may lay up to 30,000 eggs.

Average Size: 20–30 in., 10–20 lb.

Fishing Tip: Fish with large, active live bait in eddies where small streams enter the main river.

Notes: The flathead catfish is a solitary predator that feeds aggressively on live fish. It spends the days hiding in bank holes and deep pools, then prowls logjams and the shallows for prey at night. Within their native range, flatheads have been introduced to a few lakes in an attempt to control stunted panfish populations with poor results. Flatheads have not been widely introduced outside their native range.

Description: Tadpole madtom: dark olive to brown; dark line on side; large, fleshy head. Stonecat: similar but lacks dark lateral stripe and has protruding upper jaw; both species have adipose fin continuous with tail; lacks scales.

Similar Species: bullheads (pages 30–35), catfish (pages 36–41)

Stonecat

protruding upper jaw

Tadpole Madtom

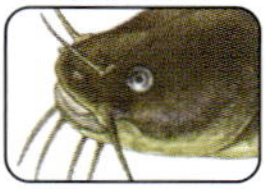

jaws even

Stonecat

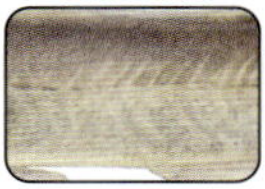

no dark lateral stripe

Tadpole Madtom

dark lateral stripe

Stonecat

fused adipose-dorsal fin

Tadpole Madtom

fused adipose-dorsal fin

Bullheads

free adipose fin

Catfish

free adipose fin

STONECAT *Noturus flavus*
TADPOLE MADTOM *Noturus gyrinus*

Other Names: willow cat

Habitat: weedy, shallow lakes; under rocks in stream riffles

Range: Stonecat: northern Missouri, Mississippi, Ohio River basin. Tadpole madtom: native to Mississippi River drainage, southeastern Gulf, and Atlantic Coast; introduced to northwest US.

Food: small invertebrates; algae and other plant matter

Reproduction: Both spawn in late spring; female lays eggs under objects such as roots, rocks, and logs or in abandoned crayfish burrows; nest and eggs are guarded by one parent.

Average Size: 3–6 in.

Fishing Tip: Reportedly, damaging the slime coating (by rolling them in sand) to make handling easier reduces their effectiveness as bait.

Notes: There are about two dozen species of madtoms, mostly found in the eastern US. All are small, secretive, nocturnal, bottom-dwelling fish. Madtoms have venom glands at the base of the dorsal and pectoral fins. Though not lethal, the venom produces a painful burning sensation. Madtoms are hardy little fish that are good bait for a wide range of game fish, from walleyes to trout.

Description: varied coloration but mostly dark gray to silver or greenish bronze; fine scales; large, deep body; large, round eye; small mouth; blunt teeth for crushing food items

Similar Species: piranha

Pacu

squarish, blunt teeth; slight underbite to overbite

Piranha

sharp, pointed teeth; pronounced underbite

BLACKFIN PACU

Colossoma macropomum

Other Names: tambaquí, black pacu, pla paku

Habitat: warm streams and rivers; weedy ponds and lakes

Range: native to the Amazon River basin; primarily Southern coastal states, with scattered records throughout US, probably aquarium releases

Food: plants and algae; opportunistic on insects, crustaceans, small fish

Reproduction: spawns in flooded wetland and forest

Average Size: 18–30 in., 5–20 lb.

Fishing Tip: Chum-feed fish with white bread, then fish dough balls near active fish.

Notes: Pacus are popular aquarium fish, and several species have been released in the US. Over 2 dozen states have records of pacus caught in the wild. They are in the same order as piranhas but are vegetarian. In warm-water states, they can grow to 35 lb. Juvenile pacus have red bellies like piranhas, possibly an adaptation to avoid predation when young (Batesian mimicry). These fast-growing fish are increasingly farmed for food.

Description: olive-to-bluish-black coloration with cream and turquoise spots; 4–6 dark blotches on sides; long, tapered dorsal and anal fins; 5–7 spines in anal fin

Similar Species: bluegill (page 238), blue tilapia (page 48)

Rio Grande Cichlid

interrupted lateral line

Bluegill

uninterrupted lateral line

Rio Grande Cichlid

5–7 anal spines

Blue Tilapia

3–4 anal spines

RIO GRANDE CICHLID

Herichthys cyanoguttatus

Other Names: Rio Grande perch, Texas cichlid, mojarra de Norta

Habitat: lakes, large springs and rivers, generally with water temperatures above 50°F

Range: native to tropical and subtropical America, northwest Mexico, and southern Texas; introduced in a number of states but established in few due to its need for warm water

Food: small fish, crustaceans, insects, fish eggs

Reproduction: Spawns in spring over rocky bottom; both parents guard eggs and young.

Average Size: 3–6 in.

Fishing Tip: Fish small jigs near channel walls.

Notes: The Rio Grande cichlid is the only North American member of this large subtropical family. It can withstand high salinities and seems to prefer canals. Rio Grande cichlids are native but are considered a destructive invasive species where they have been introduced. It's a tasty, strong fighter that is popular with a few panfish anglers.

Description: blue-gray head and body with faint dark bars; pink-to-red borders on dorsal and caudal fins; white belly; young have a dark spot on rear of dorsal fin; continuous soft- and hard-rayed dorsal fin

Similar Species: bluegill (page 238), green sunfish (page 222)

All Sunfish

blunt nose

All Tilapia

pointed nose

All Sunfish

rounded dorsal and anal fin

All Tilapia

pointed dorsal and anal fin

BLUE TILAPIA

Oreochromis aureus

Other Names: Israeli tilapia, gray bream

Habitat: warm, weedy lakes and streams; brackish and coastal salt water

Range: native to northern and western Africa and Middle East; introduced worldwide, including warmer parts of US

Food: green algae and other plankton

Reproduction: Males build small round nests and lure in females; female broods eggs in her mouth; young return to mother's mouth for protection until about 3 weeks old.

Average Size: 8–12 in., 2–3 lb.

Fishing Tip: Fish using very small balls of brightly colored PowerBait in weedbeds.

Notes: Tilapia is one of the most widely farmed fish in the world. Several species are now well established in the US and are now interbreeding, becoming hard to differentiate. The blue tilapia is the largest and most widespread species. All the tilapia compete with native species and are considered invasive and detrimental to natural habitats. Tilapia are excellent eating but, as algae eaters, are hard to get to take baited hooks. They are popular targets of bow fishers.

Description: mottled brown with creamy chin and belly; eel-like body; small barbel at each nostril opening; longer barbel on chin; long dorsal fin similar to and just above anal fin

Similar Species: bowfin (page 28), American eel (page 54), sea lamprey (page 74)

Burbot

two dorsal fins, long anal fin

Bowfin

one dorsal fin, short anal fin

American Eel

fused dorsal, tail, and anal fin

Burbot

small barbel on chin

Bowfin

no barbel on chin

Sea Lamprey

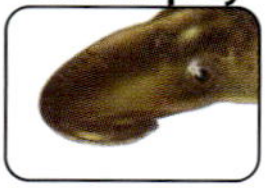

mouth: sucking disk

BURBOT

Lota lota

Other Names: lawyer, eelpout, ling, cusk

Habitat: deep, cold, clear, rock-bottomed lakes and streams

Range: northern North America into Siberia and across northern Europe

Food: primarily small fish, fish eggs, clams, and crayfish

Reproduction: Pairs to large groups spawn together in mid- to late winter; spawning occurs under the ice over a sand or gravel bottom in less than 15 feet of water; after spawning, thrashing adults scatter fertilized eggs.

Average Size: 15–20 in., 2–8 lb.

Fishing Tip: Fish with a white marabou jig tipped with a minnow near the bottom.

Notes: A member of the cod family, the burbot is a cold-water fish; it's seldom found in fisheries where the water temperature routinely exceeds 69° F. It is popular with ice fishers in some western states and Scandinavia but is considered a nuisance by most Midwestern anglers. The flesh is firm, white, and good-tasting but not popular.

Description: gray back with purple or bronze reflections; silver sides; white underbelly; humped back; dorsal fin extends from hump to near tail; lateral line runs from the head through the tail

Similar Species: white bass (page 246)

Freshwater Drum

triangular tail

White Bass

forked tail

Freshwater Drum

downturned mouth

White Bass

upturned mouth

FRESHWATER DRUM

Aplodinotus grunniens

Other Names: sheepshead, croaker, thunderpumper, grinder, bubbler; commercially marketed as white perch

Habitat: slow- to moderate-current areas of rivers and streams; shallow lakes with soft bottoms; prefers clean water but tolerates some silt

Range: from Hudson Bay through the Missouri, Mississippi, and Ohio River basins south through Mexico to Guatemala

Food: small fish, insects, crayfish, clams

Reproduction: In May and June, when water temperatures reach about 66°F, schools of drum lay eggs near the surface in open water, over sand or gravel; no parental care of fry.

Average Size: 10–15 in., 2–5 lb.

Fishing Tip: Fish with small white or yellow jigs tipped with a crayfish tail just off the bottom.

Notes: The only freshwater member of a large family of marine fish, drums are named for a grunting noise made by males, primarily to attract females. The sound is produced when specialized muscles rub along the swim bladder. The skull contains two enlarged L-shaped earstones called otoliths, once prized for jewelry by Native Americans. The flesh is flaky, white, and tasty but easily dries out when cooked.

Description: dark brown on top with yellow sides and white belly; long, snakelike body with a large mouth; gill covers; a continuous dorsal, tail, and anal fin

Similar Species: native lampreys (page 72) and sea lamprey (page 74)

American Eel

one gill cover, pectoral fins

Native Lampreys

seven gill slits, no pectoral fins

American Eel

mouth: jaws

Sea Lamprey

mouth: sucking disk

AMERICAN EEL

Anguilla rostrata

Other Names: common, Boston, Atlantic, or freshwater eel

Habitat: soft bottoms of medium-to-large streams, brackish coastal waters, open ocean

Range: Atlantic Ocean; Atlantic and Gulf drainages from Canada south to South America; most of US east of Rockies; a few introductions in the West

Food: insects, crayfish, small fish

Reproduction: A largely catadromous species, it spends most of its life in freshwater, returning to the Sargasso Sea in the North Atlantic Ocean to spawn; females lay up to 20 million eggs; adults likely die after spawning.

Average Size: 20–30 in., 2–3 lb.

Fishing Tip: At night, fish in backwaters just below dams using nightcrawlers or minnows for bait.

Notes: Leaf-shaped larval eels drift with ocean currents for about a year. When they reach river mouths of North and Central America, they morph into small eels (elvers). Males remain in the estuaries; females migrate upstream. At maturity (up to 20 years), adults return to the Sargasso Sea. Historically, eels commonly migrated up the Mississippi, Missouri, and Ohio River systems; with the many dams now in place, few eels reach very far inland.

Description: olive-to-brown body that is mottled toward the head but spotted at the rear and on rear fins; long, cylindrical profile; single dorsal fin located just above the anal fin; body encased in hard, platelike scales; broad snout; two rows of large teeth on each side of upper jaw

Similar Species: longnose gar (page 58) and spotted gar (page 62)

Alligator Gar

double row of large teeth on each side of upper jaw; no spots on head

Longnose Gar

snout twice the length of the rest of head; no spots on head

Spotted Gar

distance from front of eye to back of gill more than two-thirds snout length; spots on head

ALLIGATOR GAR

Atractosteus spatula

Other Names: garfish, spotted gar

Habitat: large warm, shallow rivers and lakes; brackish marshes, estuaries, and bays

Range: Gulf Coastal Plain from Mexico to Florida, lower reaches of Missouri, Mississippi, and Ohio Rivers; extirpated from much of its former range

Food: live and dead fish

Reproduction: Adhesive eggs are deposited in weedy shallows when water temperatures reach the high 60s; no parental care is given.

Average Size: 36–48 in., 30–60 lb.

Fishing Tip: Float large dead fish in deep, muddy river pools near incoming streams.

Notes: The alligator gar is one of the most spectacular fish in North America, reaching 8 ft. in length and 300 lbs. Like other gars, their hard mouths and sharp teeth make them hard to hook and land. Over much of their range, they are now quite rare, but a reasonable population still exists in Florida. Mostly fish eaters, they will occasionally ambush waterfowl and small mammals.

Description: olive to brown with dark spots along sides; long, cylindrical profile; single dorsal fin located just above the anal fin; body is encased in hard, platelike scales; snout twice as long as head; needle-sharp teeth on both jaws

Similar Species: shortnose gar (page 60), spotted gar (page 62)

Longnose Gar

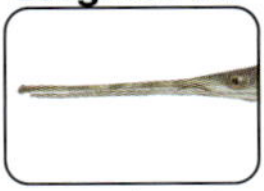

snout length 15–20 times width; no spots on head

Shortnose Gar

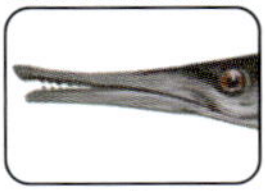

snout length about 6 times width; no spots on head

Spotted Gar

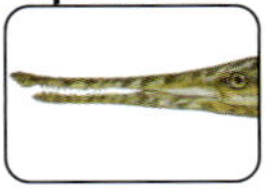

snout length about 10–12 times width; spots on head

LONGNOSE GAR

Lepisosteus osseus

Other Names: garfish

Habitat: large slow rivers and lakes; brackish inlets and shallow coastal waters

Range: Atlantic slope drainage; Mississippi and Ohio River drainages; few rivers in the Great Lakes basin; Gulf drainage from Florida to Mexico

Food: minnows and other small fish

Reproduction: Lays large green eggs in weedy shallows when water temperatures reach the high 60s; using a small disk on the snout, newly hatched gars attach to nearby plants, rocks, or branches until the digestive tract develops enough to begin feeding; the large, yellowish-green eggs are toxic to mammals.

Average Size: 24–36 in., 2–6 lb.

Fishing Tip: To catch gars, you need to entangle their teeth using spinner jigs made from frayed nylon rope.

Notes: The longnose gar belongs to a prehistoric family of fish that can breathe air with the aid of a modified swim bladder. This adaptation makes them well suited to survive in increasingly polluted rivers and lakes. They hunt by floating motionless near the surface, then making a swift sideways slash to capture prey. Longnose gars prefer warm, deep water and often school near the surface. Gars are a valuable asset in controlling the increasing populations of rough fish.

Description: olive-to-slate-green head, back, and sides; long cylindrical body; single dorsal fin located just above the anal fin; body encased in hard, platelike scales; snout one-third longer than head; needle-sharp teeth on both jaws

Similar Species: longnose gar (page 58), spotted gar (page 62)

Shortnose Gar

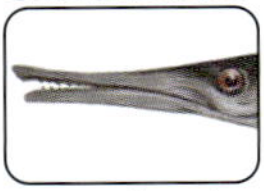

snout length about 6 times width

Longnose Gar

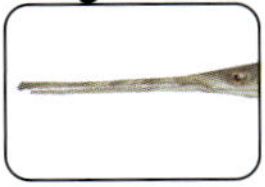

snout length about 15–20 times width

SHORTNOSE GAR

Lepisosteus platostomus

Other Names: stubnose, broadnose, or shortbilled gar

Habitat: open water of warm, slow-moving streams, backwaters, and shallow lakes

Range: low-gradient portions of Mississippi and Ohio River drainages from the southern Great Lakes to the Gulf

Food: minnows and small fish, crayfish

Reproduction: Adhesive eggs are deposited in weedy shallows when water temperatures reach the high 60s; using a small disk on the snout, newly hatched gars attach to something solid until the digestive tract develops enough to allow feeding.

Average Size: 12–24 in., 1–2 lb.

Fishing Tip: Fish near the surface with flies and jigs made from nylon rope to catch in their teeth.

Notes: Shortnose gars are not as widely dispersed as longnose gars. They prefer somewhat more active water and can tolerate higher turbidity than longnose gars. Like other gars, shortnose gars can "gulp" air and withstand very warm and poorly oxygenated water. An ambush predator, it is often seen floating near brush piles and windswept shorelines at the current's edge.

Description: back and sides olive-brown to black-tan below; brown or black spots on head, body, and fins; moderately long snout with only one row of teeth on upper jaw; dark stripes often on sides and back of young

Similar Species: longnose gar (page 58), shortnose gar (page 60)

Spotted Gar

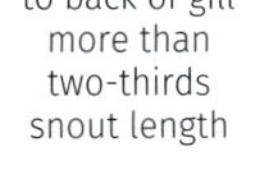

distance from front of eye to back of gill more than two-thirds snout length

Longnose Gar

snout twice the length of the rest of head

SPOTTED GAR

Lepisosteus oculatus

Other Names: garfish

Habitat: quiet water of medium-to-large rivers and lakes with good vegetation or brushy wood piles

Range: Mississippi River drainage from Gulf to eastern Great Lakes; Gulf slope drainage from Texas to western Florida

Food: minnows and other small fish

Reproduction: Adhesive eggs are deposited in weedy shallows when water temperatures reach the high 60s; using a small disk on the snout, newly hatched gars attach to something solid until the digestive tract develops enough to allow feeding.

Average Size: 18–30 in., 4–6 lb.

Fishing Tip: Drift minnows or small lures just below the surface near brush piles.

Notes: The spotted gar is the smallest of the seven gar species found in North America. All the gars can gulp air using their swim bladder as a primitive lung. Spotted gars seem to be more nocturnal than the other gars. As with the other gars, the green eggs are reported to be toxic.

Description: slate-gray scaled body with black and brown spots; steep forehead with bulging eyes; front dorsal fin tinged green with a black spot; a single scallop-shaped dorsal fin

Similar Species: mottled sculpin (page 166)

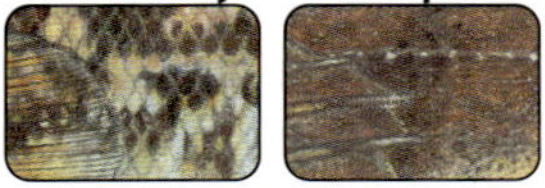

ROUND GOBY

Neogobius melanostomus

Other Names: rock goby

Habitat: rocky streams and lake shorelines; brackish coastal shorelines and tributary streams

Range: native to the Black and Caspian Seas; invasive in Northern Europe and the Great Lakes

Food: mollusks, crustaceans, insects, and fish eggs

Reproduction: Spawns several times a year in streams and along rocky shorelines; male protects eggs.

Average Size: 3–12 in.

Fishing Tip: Check bait pails carefully to ensure that gobies are not introduced to new lakes.

Notes: The round goby is an aggressively expanding invasive species that negatively impacts native species. Where it becomes established, native fish populations decrease. Introduced to the Great Lakes in the late 1980s, they are now established in the Great Lakes and its tributary streams, as well as the Finger Lakes in New York. Larger gobies are effective predators of zebra mussels, but their overall effect on lake ecology is negative.

Description: silver body and blue-gray back; three or more dark spots on the shoulder; deep and laterally compressed body; large mouth extending to back of eye; sawtooth edge of sharply pointed scales (scutes) along the belly

Similar Species: gizzard shad (page 68), threadfin shad (page 70)

Gizzard Shad	Threadfin Shad	American Shad	Hickory Shad
snout protrudes over mouth	terminal mouth	mouth extends to back of eye; jaws even	protruding lower jaw

AMERICAN SHAD

Alosa sapidissima

Other Names: river, silver, or white shad

Habitat: coastal marine most of the year, migrating up large rivers to spawn; landlocked in a few lakes

Range: Atlantic Coast and associated spawning rivers from Newfoundland to Florida; introduced to the Sacramento River on the Pacific Coast; now established on Pacific Coast and spreading north to Alaska and Russia

Food: plankton, crustaceans, small fish

Reproduction: American shad migrate up spawning rivers when water temperatures reach 62°F to 67°F; spawning takes place at night in the large rivers at the mouth of tributary streams; in the North, adults return to sea after spawning; in Southern states, they often die after spawning.

Average Size: 18–20 in., 2–3 lb.

Fishing Tip: Fish using silver spoons or bright hair jigs at the current's edge.

Notes: The American and similar hickory shad are large shad that are important to both commercial and sport fishing on the East Coast. They make spectacular spring spawning runs that reportedly saved George Washington's starving troops at Valley Forge. American shad readily take small artificial lures and are particularly popular with fly-fishers. Shad are oily fish that are very good smoked.

Description: deep, laterally compressed body; silvery-blue back with white sides and belly; young fish have a dark spot on shoulder behind the gill; small mouth; last rays of dorsal fin form a long thread

Similar Species: threadfin shad (page 70)

Threadfin Shad

terminal mouth

Gizzard Shad

snout protrudes over mouth

Threadfin Shad

yellow tail

Gizzard Shad

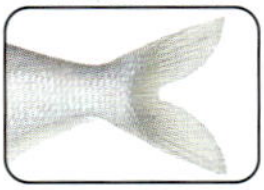

no yellow on tail

GIZZARD SHAD

Dorosoma cepedianum

Other Names: hickory, mud, or jack shad; skipjack

Habitat: large rivers, reservoirs, lakes, swamps, and temporarily flooded pools; brackish and saline waters in coastal areas

Range: St. Lawrence River and the Great Lakes; Mississippi basin; Atlantic slope drainage south to Central Florida; Gulf slope drainage into Mexico

Food: herbivorous filter feeder

Reproduction: Spawning takes place in tributary streams and along lakeshores in early summer; schooling adults release eggs in open water without regard for individual mates.

Average Size: 4–8 in., 1–8 oz.

Fishing Tip: Large gizzard shad can be caught by using wax-worms in quiet pools at the current's edge.

Notes: The gizzard shad is a widespread, prolific fish that is best known as forage for popular game fish. At times, gizzard shad can become overabundant and experience large die-offs. The name "gizzard" refers to this shad's long, convoluted intestine that is often packed with sand. Though gizzard shad are a management problem at times, they play a valuable role in turning plankton into usable forage for large game fish.

Description: silvery-yellow back with white sides and belly; dark spot on shoulder behind gill; deep, laterally compressed body; small terminal mouth; last rays of dorsal fin form a long thread

Similar Species: gizzard shad (page 68)

Threadfin Shad

terminal mouth

Gizzard Shad

snout protrudes over mouth

Threadfin Shad

yellow tail

Gizzard Shad

no yellow on tail

THREADFIN SHAD

Dorosoma petenense

Other Names: silver, yellow, or thread shad

Habitat: currents of warm, large rivers and reservoirs; brackish and saline waters in coastal areas

Range: native to lower Mississippi and Ohio River drainages; Gulf and southern Atlantic slope drainages; widely introduced as forage fish

Food: herbivorous filter feeder

Reproduction: Large schools spawn in shore shallows when water temperatures reach the low 70s; adhesive eggs are spread over vegetation and left unguarded.

Average Size: 2–5 in., 6–8 oz.

Fishing Tip: Dead or alive, shad are great catfish bait.

Notes: The threadfin shad is similar to the gizzard shad but is smaller and prefers currents in rivers and more-open water in reservoirs. It is a southern species that has spread into the central US since the 1950s. Threadfin shad are native to the southern Mississippi and Ohio River drainages but have been stocked as forage for large game fish well beyond their native range. They require warm water and die when water temperatures drop below 41° F. When the water warms in summer, they migrate upstream and can become very abundant in some areas, but after cold winters they may be very scarce.

Description: eel-like body with round, sucking-disk mouth and seven paired gill openings; dorsal fin is long, extending to the tail; no paired fins

Similar Species: sea lamprey (page 74), American eel (page 54)

Native Lampreys

mouth is a sucking disk

American Eel

mouth has jaws

Native Lampreys

undivided dorsal fin

Sea Lamprey

dorsal divided by deep notch

Native Lampreys

CHESTNUT LAMPREY *Ichthyomyzon castaneus*
AMERICAN BROOK LAMPREY *Lampetra appendix*

Other Names: lampies, wormfish

Habitat: Juveniles live in the quiet pools of streams and rivers; adults may move into lakes.

Range: freshwater throughout the US

Food: Juvenile lampreys are filter feeders in stream bottoms; adults are either parasitic on fish or do not feed.

Reproduction: Adults build nests in the gravel of streambeds, typically after water temperatures reach about 55° F; adults die shortly after spawning.

Average Size: 6–12 in., 2–8 oz.

Fishing Tip: They aren't targeted or used for bait by anglers.

Notes: There are about two dozen species of lampreys native to the US. These fish are small and secretive and not often seen. The parasitic ones leave a small, visible sore on the host fish's side after feeding. Native lampreys coexist with other native fish species with little or no effect on their populations. The lampreys are some of the oldest vertebrates, with fossil records dating back 500 million years.

Description: eel-like body; round, sucking-disk mouth; seven paired gill openings; dorsal fin extends to the tail and is divided into two sections by a deep notch; no paired fins

Similar Species: native lampreys (page 72) and American eel (page 54)

Sea Lamprey

mouth is a sucking disk

American Eel

mouth has jaws

Sea Lamprey

dorsal divided by deep notch

Native Lampreys

undivided dorsal fin

SEA LAMPREY

Petromyzon marinus

Other Names: landlocked lamprey, lake lamprey

Habitat: Juveniles live in quiet pools of freshwater streams; adults are free-swimming in lakes and oceans.

Range: Atlantic Ocean from Greenland to Florida, Norway to the Mediterranean; landlocked in the Great Lakes and several New York lakes

Food: Juveniles are filter feeders in the bottoms of streams; the adult is parasitic on fish, attaching itself using its disk-shaped sucker mouth, then using its sharp tongue to rasp through the fish's scales and skin to feed on blood and bodily fluids.

Reproduction: Both adults build a nest in the gravel of a clear stream, then die shortly after spawning; young remain in streams several years before returning to the lake as adults.

Average Size: 12–24 in., 0.5–2 lbs.

Fishing Tip: Do not return sea lampreys to the lake.

Notes: Native to the Atlantic Ocean, the sea lamprey coexisted with native species until it became landlocked in the Great Lakes. It was initially blocked by waterfalls, but the building of the Erie Canal (1825) and the Welland Canal (1919) allowed it to reach the Great Lakes, where it became established and reproduced without returning to the sea. Soon after, lake trout and whitefish populations declined. Control measures such as traps and chemicals have reduced sea lamprey numbers, allowing native fish populations to slowly recover.

Description: silver-to-olive-green back and sides; scales outlined, giving sides a cross-hatched appearance; upturned mouth; dark bar under eye; rounded tail fin; long, pointed anal fin on males; small, rounded anal fin on females

Similar Species: fathead minnow (page 94)

Fathead Minnow

mouth not upturned, no bar under eye

Mosquitofish

terminal mouth, bar under eye

Fathead Minnow

forked tail

Mosquitofish

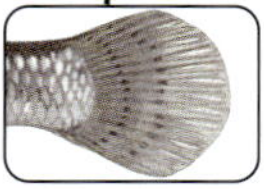

female has spots on tail

MOSQUITOFISH

Gambusia holbrooki

Other Names: mosquito minnow, surface minnow

Habitat: surface of well-vegetated backwaters with little current and protected from the wind; can survive high temperatures and salinity and low oxygen levels

Range: native to southern Mississippi River drainage; Gulf and southern Atlantic slope drainages; introduced worldwide

Food: insects, crustaceans, and some plant material

Reproduction: Females give birth to live young after internal fertilization; may produce several broods in a single season.

Average Size: 2–3 in.

Fishing Tip: They are not hardy enough for bait.

Notes: There are only about 20 species in the livebearer family in the US, but it is a well-represented family in subtropical and tropical America. Mosquitofish have been widely introduced worldwide to control mosquitos but seem to be no better at it than native species. Their upturned mouth is an adaption for attacking from below to catch insects that land on the water surface.

Description: dark-gray-to-black back; silver-gray sides with dark blotches; low-set eyes; upturned mouth; tiny body scales (none on head)

Similar Species: common carp (page 82), silver carp (page 80), grass carp (page 84)

Bighead Carp

small silver scales

Common Carp

large yellow scales with a dark margin

Grass Carp

large silver scales with a dark margin

Silver Carp

small silver scales

Bighead Carp

keeled belly from pelvic fin to anal fin

Silver Carp

keeled belly from gills to anal fin

Bighead/Silver Carp

eyes low on head

Common Carp

eyes high on head

BIGHEAD CARP

Hypophthalmichthys nobilis

Other Names: river carp, lake fish, speckled amur

Habitat: large, warm rivers and connected lakes

Range: Asia; introduced to the Missouri, Mississippi, and Ohio River basins and spreading

Food: aquatic vegetation and floating plankton, mostly algae

Reproduction: Adults spawn from late spring to early summer in warm, flowing water.

Average Size: 15–30 in., 5–50 lb.

Fishing Tip: As filter feeders, bighead carp are targets for bow fishermen but not anglers. They reportedly can be caught with wet flies.

Notes: Bighead carp are the fourth-most important aquaculture fish in the world. They were introduced to the US to control algae in southern aquaculture ponds and escaped to the Mississippi River. They are now well established in the lower Mississippi and Ohio River systems. The silver carp and, to a lesser degree, the bighead carp make high leaps from the water when frightened by boats. They have a pleasant, mild flavor but are bony and not highly regarded as table fare in this country. There is concern that bighead carp will become established in the Great Lakes and do great harm to the native species populations.

Description: dark-green back; silver sides with a cross-hatched pattern; upturned mouth; eyes far forward and low on head; tiny troutlike scales; no scales on head

Similar Species: bighead carp (page 78), common carp (page 82), grass carp (page 84)

Silver Carp

small silver scales

Bighead Carp

small silver scales

Common Carp

large yellow scales with dark margin

Grass Carp

large silver scales with dark margin

Silver Carp

keeled belly from gills to anal fin

Bighead Carp

keeled belly from pelvic fin to anal fin

Silver/Bighead Carp

eyes low on head, mouth lacks barbels

Common Carp

eyes high on head, mouth has barbels

SILVER CARP

Hypophthalmichthys molitrix

Other Names: shiner carp

Habitat: quiet waters of large, warm rivers and connected lakes and ponds

Range: native to Asia; introduced to many other parts of the world, including the Missouri, Mississippi, and Ohio River basins in the US; expanding into some of the Great Lake drainages

Food: floating algae and small aquatic vegetation

Reproduction: Adults spawn from late spring to early summer in backwaters of large to midsize streams.

Average Size: 20–30 in., 5–20 lb.

Fishing Tip: Algae feeders, they are targets for bow fishers but not anglers. Reportedly, they can be caught on hook and line by floating small baits, like waxworms, in feeding schools.

Notes: Silver carp were introduced to Arkansas in the early 1970s to control algae in aquaculture ponds and sewage lagoons, then escaped to the Mississippi River. Large breeding populations are well established in the Ohio, Illinois, and lower Mississippi Rivers. Combined with bighead carp, they are the predominant fish in some areas and have had a very negative effect on river ecology. They have limited food value in this country but are an important food source in other parts of the world. The silver carp and, to a lesser degree, the bighead carp make high leaps from the water when frightened by boats.

Description: back and sides brassy yellow to dark olive; whitish-yellow belly; round mouth has two pairs of barbels; reddish tail and anal fin; dark margin on each scale

Similar Species: bighead carp (page 78), silver carp (page 80), grass carp (page 84)

Common Carp

large yellow scales with dark margin

Bighead/Silver Carp

small silver scales

Grass Carp

large silver scales with dark margin

Common Carp

eyes high on head

Bighead/Silver Carp

eyes low on head

COMMON CARP

Cyprinus carpio

Other Names: German carp, European carp, Mirror carp, Leather carp, buglemouth

Habitat: warm, shallow, quiet, well-vegetated waters of streams and lakes

Range: native to Eurasia; introduced throughout the world, including North America south of the 50th parallel

Food: opportunistic feeder; prefers insect larvae, crustaceans, and mollusks but at times eats algae and some higher plants

Reproduction: Adults spawn from late spring to early summer in very shallow water at stream and lake edges; very obvious when spawning, with a great deal of splashing.

Average Size: 3–15 lb., 18–24 in.

Fishing Tip: For big carp, fish shallow vegetation at night.

Notes: The carp is one of the world's most important freshwater fish. This fast-growing fish has provided sport and food for millions of people for many centuries. This Asian minnow was introduced into Europe in the 1200s but didn't make it to North America until 1877. Carp are a highly prized sport fish in Europe, but they have not gained the same status in the US, even though some line and bow fishers do enthusiastically fish for carp.

Description: silver-gray head and sides with a golden-green sheen; grayish-green fins; large scales; eyes set in middle of head; terminal mouth; torpedo-shaped body not as deep as common carp

Similar Species: common carp (page 82)

Grass Carp

mouth upturned, no barbels, eye low on head

Common Carp

downturned mouth with barbels, eye high on head

GRASS CARP

Ctenopharyngodon idella

Other Names: white amur, silver carp, or weed carp

Habitat: warm, shallow, quiet, weedy waters of streams and lakes

Range: native to western Siberia and Asia; introduced to 20 countries and 35 US states; widespread in lower and middle Mississippi River Valley

Food: aquatic vegetation

Reproduction: Adults spawn in streams where eggs are released and fertilized in a slow current; only stocked as non-reproducing, sterile fish.

Average Size: 24–30 in., 5 –20 lb.

Fishing Tip: Fish using small dough baits just off the bottom in weedbeds.

Notes: Grass carp were first introduced to the US in 1961 by the U.S. Fish and Wildlife Service to control aquatic vegetation. It was soon learned that by exposing the eggs to heat, sterile fish could be produced. These sterile fish are now widely stocked for weed control in artificial lakes. Grass carp do not take bait readily, but a few escaped fish are caught by anglers. Fish caught in posted vegetation-control areas should be released so they can go about their job of weed control; in all other areas, they should be removed.

Description: dark olive green on back fading to copper on sides and belly; football-shaped body; small barbel at corner of mouth; small scales: small red-orange eye; square tail

Similar Species: common carp (page 82)

Common Carp

large scales

Tench

small scales

Common Carp

forked tail

Tench

square tail

TENCH

Tinca tinca

Other Names: doctor fish, slime fish, carp minnow

Habitat: still water in lakes and streams with muddy bottom and thick vegetation

Range: native to northern Europe and Asia; recorded in 38 states across US, well established in several Western states

Food: small snails, clams, insect larvae, some algae

Reproduction: Female lays sticky green eggs that attach to vegetation in shallow water with muddy bottom; mature female may lay 300,000 eggs; no parental care is given.

Average Size: 2–5 lb., 12–20 in.

Fishing Tip: At night, fish with small worms on the bottom in shallow water with scattered vegetation.

Notes: Tench were introduced into the United States in 1877 by the U.S. Forest Service and are now well established in some streams and lakes. Tench are abundant in some waters but not nearly as widespread as the common carp. They can survive in very muddy water with low oxygen levels that are near freezing. Tench rooting in shallow mud can be very disruptive for spawning native species.

Description: dark-olive back; silver-gray sides that reflect purple; large mouth; dark spot at base of dorsal fin; small barbel that fits in a groove between the back of the upper jaw and snout (very evident when mouth is open)

Similar Species: common shiner (page 98) and golden shiner (page 98)

Creek Chub

mouth extends to eye

Shiners

mouth does not extend to eye

CREEK CHUB

Semotilus atromaculatus

Other Names: common, brook, silver, mud, or blackspot chub; horned or northern horned dace

Habitat: clear streams and rivers; occasionally lakes

Range: Missouri, Mississippi, and Ohio River drainages; northern New Mexico

Food: small aquatic invertebrates and crustaceans

Reproduction: In late spring, male excavates a 1- to 3-foot-long, teardrop-shaped pit at the head of stream riffles; using its mouth or rolling stones with its head, male fills pit to 6–8 inches high; female lays eggs on the mound; male covers and defends eggs. Several other species spawn on the mounds, occasionally resulting in hybridization.

Average Size: 4–10 in., 3–8 oz.

Fishing Tip: Creek chubs can be caught with hook and line using very small baits.

Notes: Creek chubs are one of the most common fish in clear streams of the central and eastern US. When water levels are low, spawning mounds can be plentiful and quite evident, leaving many to speculate on their origan. Chubs are highly prized bait minnows, and local populations can be easily depleted by overharvesting.

Description: black back; dark-olive sides; side scales have a black triangular bar on the front corner; large mouth; small barbel fits in a grove between back of upper jaw and snout

Similar Species: creek chub (page 88) and fathead minnow (page 94)

Fallfish

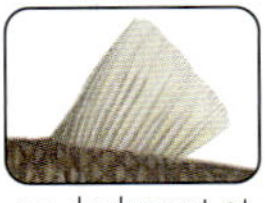

no dark spot at base of dorsal

Creek Chub

dark spot at front of dorsal

Fathead Minnow

dark spot at front of dorsal

Fallfish

pointed tail

Creek Chub

rounded tail

Fathead Minnow

rounded tail

FALLFISH

Semotilus corporalis

Other Names: windfish, silver chub

Habitat: quiet pools in clear streams; lake shorelines

Range: Atlantic slope drainage

Food: aquatic invertebrates and crustaceans

Reproduction: In late spring, male builds a spectacular nest by carrying or rolling stones into a mound up to 6 feet long and 3 feet high; several females lay eggs on the mound; eggs are guarded by the male.

Average Size: 8–15 in., 6–15 oz.

Fishing Tip: Drift small plastic grub jigs out of the current into deep pools.

Notes: The fallfish is the largest native minnow east of the Appalachians and one of the most abundant fish in many streams. They build amazing nest mounds that are very visible when water levels are low. Not as prestigious as trout, fallfish have a strong following among fly and ultralight fishers.

Description: moderately dark back; two broad lateral bands on tan background; in breeding males, the tan turns orange, and the belly becomes bright red or orange; blunt nose

Similar Species: creek chub (page 88) and fathead minnow (page 94)

Northern Redbelly Dace

curved mouth; lower jaw slightly ahead of upper

Creek Chub

mouth extends almost to middle of eye

Fathead Minnow

upturned mouth does not extend to eye

NORTHERN REDBELLY DACE

Phoxinus eos

Other Names: redbelly, leatherback, yellow-belly dace

Habitat: small streams, bog, and lakes

Range: Atlantic drainages from New England through the upper Missouri River drainage; northwest through the Peace and Mackenzie River drainages of Canada

Food: plant material

Reproduction: From May to early August, a single female accompanied by several males will dart among masses of filamentous algae laying 5–30 non-adhesive eggs at a time; males fertilize the eggs, which hatch in 8–10 days with no parental care.

Average Size: 2–3 in.

Fishing Tip: Dace are average as bait minnows. They survive in the bait pail pretty well but not long once on the hook.

Notes: There are a half dozen dace species of minnows in North America. Dace are small fish, often brightly colored, that live in a variety of habitats. The northern redbelly dace is a hardy fish often found in the acidic water of bogs, beaver ponds, and darkly stained lakes and less frequently in small streams. Breeding males are one of the US's most brightly colored fish and surpass many aquarium fish in beauty. Northern redbelly dace often hybridize with other species and sometimes form all-female populations.

Description: Bluntnose: yellow-brown back; silver sides with a cross-hatched appearance; dusky line from snout to tail, ending in a dark spot; Fathead: olive back; golden-yellow sides without cross-hatching; faded line from gills to tail (bright in breeding males), ending in a dark spot

Similar Species: redbelly dace (page 92) and creek chub (page 88)

Fathead Minnow

upturned mouth does not extend to eye

Creek Chub

downturned mouth extends to eye

Fathead Minnow

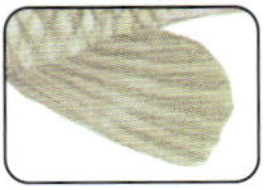

anal fin has 7 rays

Creek Chub

anal fin has 8 rays

BLUNTNOSE MINNOW *Pimephales notatus*
FATHEAD MINNOW *Pimephales promelas*

Other Names: spottail minnow, blackhead minnow, or tuffy minnow

Habitat: streams, ponds, and lakes, particularly shallow, weedy, turbid areas lacking many predators

Range: found in most of North America from Chihuahua, Mexico, north to Great Slave Lake, Canada; widely introduced from bait pail releases

Food: primarily herbivorous but will eat insects and copepods

Reproduction: Spawns spring through late summer when water temperatures reach 60°F; male prepares nest under rocks and sticks; female enters, turns upside down, and lays adhesive eggs on the overhead object; after female leaves, male fertilizes the eggs, then guards, fans with its fins, and massages with a special mucuslike pad on its back.

Average Size: 1–2 in.

Fishing Tip: Some anglers report less luck when using breeding male fatheads as bait, perhaps due to their color or a differing scent.

Notes: Minnows are small fish, not the young of larger species. The fathead and bluntnose are two of the most numerous and widespread of the 200 minnow species in the US. They are widely farmed to be used as bait. Both are hardy and withstand extremely low oxygen levels in the wild and in bait buckets. These bait minnows are two of the most economically important fish in the US.

Description: variable color; can be green, red, orange, gold, pink, or a variegated black and orange; deep body; fins heavy and rounded; dorsal fin originates just above or behind pectoral fins

Similar Species: common carp (page 82)

Goldfish

no chin barbels

Common Carp

chin barbels

Goldfish

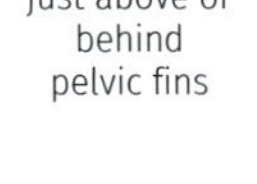

dorsal fin originates just above or behind pelvic fins

Common Carp

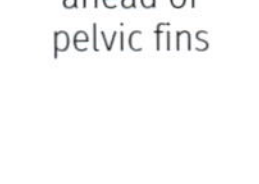

dorsal fin originates just ahead of pelvic fins

GOLDFISH

Carassius auratus

Other Names: golden carp; Indiana, Baltimore, or Missouri minnow

Habitat: quiet, well-vegetated streams; weedy lake edges

Range: native from Eastern Europe to Asia; introduced worldwide, including in the US

Food: scavenges both plant and animal matter

Reproduction: Its long spawning season lasts from late spring through summer; spawns in very shallow water at stream and lake edges; very sticky eggs are spread over vegetation; no parental care is given.

Average Size: 3–10 in., 4–12 oz.

Fishing Tip: Though it makes a good, strong baitfish, it's not legal to use in some states.

Notes: Goldfish have been reported throughout the US and are common in some areas but are infrequently becoming abundant enough to pose a problem. Goldfish often hybridize with common carp and through a unique fertilization process sometimes form all-female populations. Brightly colored goldfish are very susceptible to predation, so most wild populations are darker colored.

Description: Golden: deep, slab-sided, gold body; lateral line is a pronounced downward curve. Common: thin silver body; breeding males have a pinkish body and fin.

Similar Species: creek chub (page 88)

Common Shiner

8–10 rays on anal fin (usually 9)

Golden Shiner

11–15 rays on anal fin

Common Shiner

eye large in relation to the head

COMMON SHINER *Luxilus cornutus*
GOLDEN SHINER *Notemigonus crysoleucas*

Other Names: bream, roach, butterfish, pond shiner, creek shiner

Habitat: well-vegetated lakes and stream pools

Range: Missouri, Mississippi, and Ohio River drainages through the East; widely introduced in the West

Food: aquatic insects, small crustaceans, and mollusks

Reproduction: Golden spreads eggs over shallow vegetation. Common builds small rocky nest.

Average Size: 3–12 in.

Fishing Tip: Both can be caught with small flies or small bits of worms.

Notes: There over a hundred minnows called shiners in North America, and many are hard to tell apart. Not all are flashy, as the name indicates; some are dull, with little shine. Both the common and golden get big enough to eat but are not as tasty or meaty as panfish. Widely used as a baitfish, the more popular golden shiner seems to be a little less hardy on the hook.

Description: back is olive-green to silver-blue; silver sides; white underside; metallic-blue coloration with bright orange-red on the head and fins (except dorsal) on breeding males

Similar Species: golden shiner (page 98) and creek chub (page 88)

Red Shiner

9 rays on anal fin

Golden Shiner

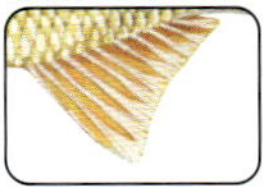

11–15 rays on anal fin

Shiners

mouth barely extends to eye

Creek Chub

mouth extends almost to middle of eye

RED SHINER

Cyprinella lutrensis

Other Names: silver shiner, silver fish, silver minnow

Habitat: slow-moving streams with deeper pools; impoundments

Range: native to Mississippi River and Gulf drainages into Mexico; introduced to Colorado River basin, expanding east

Food: algae, zoo plankton, small invertebrates

Reproduction: It spawns in late spring to early summer when water temperature reaches lower 60s; spawns in a variety of habitats but prefers vegetated or brushy pools over gravel beds; occasionally spawns on the edge of empty sunfish nests.

Average Size: 1–3 in.

Fishing Tip: This is a hardy bait minnow.

Notes: This schooling fish frequents the middle of the water column to the surface. Red shiners are tolerant of polluted, silty water and are becoming the dominant minnow in some degraded urban streams. They are considered an invasive species outside their native range, displacing or hybridizing with native species.

Description: back and upper sides dark green to dark blue; bright silver or golden sides; large yellow-tinged eye; large scales; thin body flattened from side to side with a sharp, scaled ridge (keel) from throat to pelvic fin; forward-facing mouth with small teeth

Similar Species: mooneye (page 104), gizzard shad (page 68)

Goldeye

leading edge of dorsal fin even with or behind anal fin

Mooneye

leading edge of dorsal fin ahead of anal fin

Goldeye

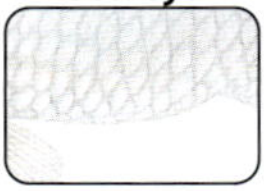

fleshy keel

Gizzard Shad

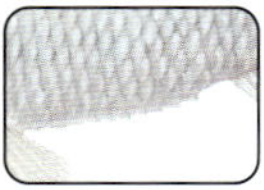

scaled, sawlike keel

GOLDEYE

Hiodon alosoides

Other Names: Winnipeg or western goldeye; toothed or yellow herring

Habitat: large lakes and quiet backwaters of large, turbid streams and rivers

Range: lower Mississippi and Missouri basins; throughout Great Plains and northwestern Canada

Food: insects, small fish, crayfish, snails

Reproduction: Spawning takes place in turbid pools and backwaters when water temperatures reach the mid-50s.

Average Size: 10–17 in., 8–20 oz.

Fishing Tip: While not often an angler's target, goldeyes readily take flies and small jigs.

Notes: The goldeye's large yellow eye is an adaptation for low-light conditions that enables it to feed at night and navigate dark, silty waters. They feed near the surface in quiet pools and are often found with mooneyes. Harvested commercially from large Canadian lakes for 150 years, they were served on the Canadian Pacific Railway as Winnipeg-smoked goldeye. They are still fairly common in the Mississippi and Missouri Rivers.

Description: silver with an olive back; large scales on the body but none on the head; large white eye more than one-third the width of head; thin body with a sharp, scaleless keel between pelvic and anal fins

Similar Species: goldeye (page 102), gizzard shad (page 68)

Mooneye

leading edge of dorsal fin ahead of anal fin

Goldeye

leading edge of dorsal fin even with or behind anal fin

Mooneye

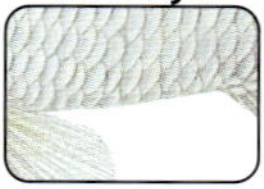

fleshy keel

Gizzard Shad

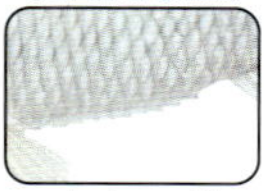

scaled, sawlike keel

MOONEYE

Hiodon tergisus

Other Names: white shad, slicker, toothed herring, river whitefish

Habitat: clear, quiet waters of large lakes and the backwaters of large streams

Range: Mississippi River and Mobile Bay drainages; most of Great Lakes Basin north to Hudson Bay

Food: insects, small fish, crayfish, snails

Reproduction: Spawning takes place in clear backwaters and over rocks in areas with fast-moving water when water temperatures reach the mid-50s; a single female may release up to 20,000 gelatin-covered eggs.

Average Size: 10–12 in., 12–16 oz.

Fishing Tip: Mooneyes will take flies, small spinners, and jigs, but they are not great fighters.

Notes: The mooneye is a flashy fish that jumps repeatedly when hooked. Like goldeyes, it is bony with little meat except along the back but is very good smoked. It commonly feeds on insects at or near the surface in slack waters of large lakes and rivers. Mooneyes prefer cleaner water than goldeyes and are becoming less common due to the siltation of many streams. Though small, it is related to the South American Arapaima, the world's largest scaled freshwater fish.

Description: olive-green back; tan-to-yellow-brown sides with faint wavy vertical bars; rounded tail; dark bar just before the tail; slightly flattened head

Similar Species: logperch (page 114), Johnny darter (page 112), fathead minnow (page 94)

Central Mudminnow

single dorsal fin

Logperch

two dorsal fins

Central Mudminnow

terminal mouth

Logperch

large mouth overhung by conical snout

Central Mudminnow

rounded tail

Fathead Minnow

forked tail

CENTRAL MUDMINNOW

Umbra limi

Other Names: Mississippi or western mudminnow; dogfish, mudfish

Habitat: slow, stagnant waters of weedy streams and ponds with soft bottoms

Range: upper Mississippi River and Great Lakes drainages

Food: insects, mollusks, larger crustaceans

Reproduction: In the early spring, adults move into flooded pools when water temperatures reach the mid-50s; yellow-orange eggs are deposited singly on plant leaves and are left to hatch without parental care.

Average Size: 2–4 in.

Fishing Tip: Mudminnows are a good bait minnow but hard to collect in any numbers.

Notes: This hardy little fish can stand very low oxygen levels and gulp air to breathe (even from air bubbles under the ice). They hide in the bottom detritus but do not bury themselves tail-first in the mud, as often reported. They are frequently the only fish left in ponds after winter die-offs. They are good baitfish, withstanding the bait pail and hooks well. They can be fun aquarium fish, quickly learning to eat small pieces of meat or angleworms when offered.

Description: blue-black back fading to silver sides and silvery-white belly; small, forward-facing mouth; dark spot at the base of pectoral fins, which are set high on sides; no visible lateral line

Similar Species: American shad (page 66)

Mullets

upturned mouth

Quillback/ Carpsuckers

sucker mouth

Mullets

two dorsal fins

Shads

single dorsal fin

STRIPED MULLET

Mugil cephalus

Other Names: black or jumping mullet

Habitat: marine and estuarine environments ascending far up coastal rivers

Range: worldwide circumtropical; Pacific, Gulf, and Atlantic coastal streams

Food: zooplankton, crustaceans, algae, organic debris

Reproduction: Spawning takes place in open seas near inlets or along beaches in fall or early winter.

Average Size: 10–20 in., 1–3 lb.

Fishing Tip: Fish using a small hook baited with a dough ball below a large gob of chicken food and oatmeal mix stuck to the line above it.

Notes: Striped mullet is primarily a shallow salt- and brackish-water fish but can be found offshore and far up coastal streams. They are often seen making high leaps out of the water. Mullet are bony but considered fine table fare over most of their range; they take on an oily taste in some waters. Dead or alive, mullet are a very popular baitfish.

Description: large gray, scaleless body; snout protrudes into a large paddle; sharklike forked tail; gill cover extends into long, pointed flaps

Similar Species: channel catfish (page 38) and blue catfish (page 36)

Paddlefish	Channel Catfish	Blue Catfish
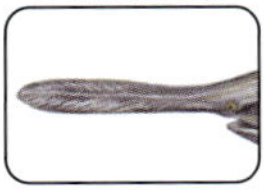		
paddlelike snout	lacks paddlelike snout	lacks paddlelike snout

PADDLEFISH

Polyodon spathula

Other Names: spoonbill cat, duckbill

Habitat: deep pools of large rivers and their connecting lakes

Range: native to Missouri, Mississippi, and Ohio River drainages; Gulf slope from East Texas to western Florida; current range much restricted

Food: free-swimming plankton

Reproduction: Spawning takes place in the spring with rising water levels; adults migrate from lakes and rivers into streams; breeding schools gather to release eggs over large gravel bars, typically in less than 10 feet of water.

Average Size: 24–36 in., 20–40 lb.

Fishing Tip: Paddlefish are legally caught by snagging in some states.

Notes: This prehistoric fish is very sharklike in terms of anatomy. Its only close relative is found in China's Yangtze River. The paddlefish has a large mouth but no teeth and feeds entirely on plankton. The function of its namesake paddle is not well understood, but it is not used to dig in the mud. Scientists believe special sensors in the snout help the paddlefish detect tiny electrical currents created by the plankton on which it feeds. With dam construction, increased pollution, and silting-in, the paddlefish is now rare over much of its native range. Both the eggs and flesh were once harvested commercially.

Description: Iowa darter: brown back with faint blotches; sides have 9–12 vertical bars; dark spot under eye; bars are more pronounced and colors brighter in breeding males. Johnny darter: tan-to-olive back and upper sides with dark blotches and speckling; sides tan to golden with X, Y, and W patterns; breeding males dark with black bars.

Similar Species: logperch (page 114)

Iowa Darter

blotchy bars on sides

Johnny Darter

X, Y, and W markings on sides

Logperch

distinct vertical bars

Darters

small mouth, blunt nose

Logperch

large mouth overhung by conical snout

IOWA DARTER *Etheostoma exile*
JOHNNY DARTER *Etheostoma nigrum*

Other Names: red-sided darter, yellowbelly darter, or weed darter

Habitat: Iowa darters inhabit slow-flowing streams and lakes that have some vegetation or an algae mat; Johnny darters are found in most rivers and streams and some lakes.

Range: upper Missouri, Mississippi, Ohio River and Great Lakes drainages extending into the Great Plains and into Canada north to Hudson Bay

Food: insect larvae, small crustaceans, mollusks

Reproduction: In May and June, males migrate to shorelines to establish breeding areas; females move from territory to territory, spawning with several males; each sequence produces 7–10 eggs, which sink and attach to the bottom.

Average Size: 2–4 in.

Fishing Tip: Neither species is a good bait minnow.

Notes: There are over 100 species of darters in the US, all related to the much larger yellow perch and walleye. There are both lake and stream darters that mostly live among the rocks where there is some current. Having a small swim bladder allows them to sink rapidly to the bottom after making a quick "dart," thus avoiding being swept away by the current. They are hard to see when still but easy to spot when making a quick dart to a new resting place, where they perch on their pectoral fins. Brightly colored darters make fine aquarium fish but require live food.

Description: back is yellowish brown to olive; lighter sides with 15–25 dark vertical bands; prominent dark spot at base of tail; pointed snout; long, cylindrical body

Similar Species: Johnny darter (page 112)

Logperch

larger mouth overhung by conical snout

Darters

small terminal mouth, blunt nose

Logperch

dark vertical bars on sides

Johnny Darter

X, Y, and W markings on sides

LOGPERCH

Percina carprodes

Other Names: log or manitou darter; zebra fish; rockfish

Habitat: large lakes and rivers

Range: native to Missouri, Mississippi, and Ohio River and Great Lakes drainages west of the Appalachians; northeast through central Canada to James Bay; introduced east of the Appalachians

Food: small aquatic invertebrates and algae

Reproduction: In late spring, adults move to the shallows; males form small mating schools (10–15 fish) that hover around a single female; adhesive eggs are deposited at random on sand; no parental care is given.

Average Size: 3–6 in.

Fishing Tip: They are not hardy enough in the bucket or on the hook to be good bait minnows.

Notes: The logperch is the most widespread and largest of the darters. They are sometimes caught by fishers netting bait or casting for panfish. When caught, they are frequently mistaken for small perch. Logperch are common prey for game fish prowling the shallows but are not good bait fish. They are showy and active and make good aquarium fish but need live food.

Description: slender body is gray-to-dark silver or yellowish brown with dark blotches on sides; black spots on spiny dorsal fin; may exhibit some white on lower margin of tail but lacks prominent white spot found on walleyes

Similar Species: walleye (page 118), saugeye

Sauger

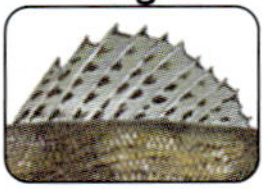

dorsal has distinct circular spots, no blotch on rear base

Saugeye

dorsal has distinct spots and blotch at rear base

Walleye

dorsal has indistinct spots, dark blotch on rear base

Sauger

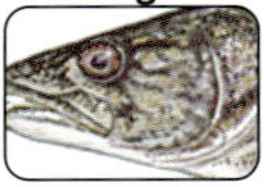

cheeks rough with few scales

Saugeye

cheeks rough with scales

Walleye

cheeks smooth with few scales

SAUGER

Sander canadensis

Other Names: sand pike, spotfin pike, river pike, jackfish, jack salmon

Habitat: large lakes and rivers

Range: native to Missouri, Mississippi, and Ohio River and Great Lakes drainages west of the Appalachians; northeast through central Canada to James Bay; introduced east of the Appalachians

Food: small fish, aquatic insects, crayfish

Reproduction: Adults spawn in April and May as water approaches 50° F; adults move into the shallow waters of tributaries and headwaters to randomly deposit eggs over gravel beds.

Average Size: 10–15 in., .5–2 lb.

Fishing Tip: Saugers are slightly more aggressive daytime feeders compared to walleyes and respond to a little faster retrieve and brighter colors during summer river fishing.

Notes: Though the sauger is the walleye's smaller cousin, it is a big-water fish primarily found in large lakes and rivers. It is slow-growing, often reaching only 2 pounds in 20 years. In nature, walleyes occasionally hybridize with saugers, producing a saugeye. Saugeyes (female walleye x male sauger) are popular for stocking programs.

Description: long, round body; dark silver or golden to dark olive-brown in color; spines in both first dorsal and anal fin; sharp canine teeth; dark spot at base of the three last spines in the dorsal fin; white spot on bottom lobe of tail

Similar Species: sauger and saugeye (page 116)

Walleye	**Sauger**	**Saugeye**
	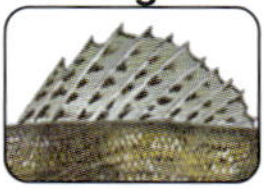	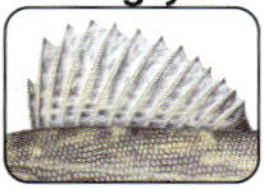
spiny dorsal with indistinct spots and dark blotch on rear base	spiny dorsal with distinct spots and no blotch on rear base	spiny dorsal with distinct spots and dark blotch on rear base
Walleye	**Sauger**	**Saugeye**

white spot on bottom lobe of tail	no white spot on bottom of tail	no white spot on bottom of tail

WALLEYE

Sander vitreus

Other Names: marble-eyes, 'eye, walter, walleyed pike, jack, jackfish, pickerel

Habitat: lakes, rivers, and streams; abundant in some very large lakes

Range: native to upper Missouri, Mississippi, Ohio River and Great Lakes drainages through central Canada; widely introduced

Food: mainly small fish, insects, crayfish, leeches, and frogs

Reproduction: Spawning takes place in tributary streams or rocky lake shoals when spring water temperatures reach 45° F– 50° F; no parental care is given.

Average Size: 10–18 in., 1–3 lb.

Fishing Tip: Casting imitation crawfish lures (the kind used for bass) into rocky shorelines at night can be very effective for large walleyes.

Notes: The walleye is the most popular game fish in many Northern states and often part of stocking programs. A dogged opponent but not a spectacular fighter or jumper, the walleye is considered one of the best-tasting game fish. A reflective layer of pigment in the eye (tapetum lucidum) allows walleyes and saugers to see well in low-light conditions. As a result, walleyes are most active at dusk, at dawn, at night, and under reduced-light conditions such as choppy waves and cloudy skies.

Description: 6–9 dark, vertical bars on a background of bright yellowish green to orange; long dorsal fin with 2 distinct lobes; lower fins have a yellow-to-orange tinge

Similar Species: trout-perch (page 260), walleye (page 118)

Yellow Perch

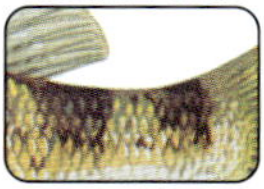

no adipose fin

Trout-Perch

adipose fin

Yellow Perch

lacks prominent white spot on tail

Walleye

prominent white spot on tail

YELLOW PERCH

Perca flavescens

Other Names: ringed, striped, or jack perch; green hornet

Habitat: lakes and streams; prefers clear, open water

Range: native to upper Missouri and Mississippi River and Great Lakes basins; Atlantic coastal drainage, northwest through Canada to James Bay; introduced in the West

Food: small fish, insects, snails, leeches, crayfish

Reproduction: Spawning takes place at night in shallow, weedy areas soon after ice-out, when water warms to 45°F; female drapes gelatinous ribbons of eggs over submerged vegetation.

Average Size: 6–10 in., 6–10 oz.

Fishing Tip: Perch are very sensitive to color, so when fishing is slow, consider changing jig color.

Notes: The yellow perch is very common and is prolific in large north-central US lakes. Small bait-stealing fish are considered a nuisance, but perch of 10 inches or more are popular with anglers. Perch are commercially harvested in some of the Great Lakes. They travel in schools of about the same age class and size, so when a group of actively feeding fish is located, large numbers can often be caught. Perch are an important link in the food web, serving as forage for large sport fish. In turn, overfishing perch can lead to a population of stunted or undersized larger predators.

Description: back and sides olive-green to yellow-brown; yellow-green chainlike markings on the sides; distinct dark teardrop below the eye; scales on the entire cheek and gill covers; fins almost clear

Similar Species: grass pickerel (page 124), northern pike (page 128), redfin pickerel (page 126)

Chain Pickerel

vertical bar under eye

Grass Pickerel

bar under eye angled backward

Northern Pike

no vertical bar under eye

Redfin Pickerel

bar under eye angled backward

Chain Pickerel

chainlike marks on sides

Grass Pickerel

lacks distinct chain marks

Redfin Pickerel

lacks distinct chain marks

CHAIN PICKEREL

Esox niger

Other Names: weed pike

Habitat: shallow, weedy lakes and sluggish streams

Range: Mississippi and upper Ohio River and eastern Great Lakes drainages; Gulf Coastal Plain from the Mississippi River to Florida

Food: small fish, frogs, and insects

Reproduction: Spawning takes place in April and May just as the ice goes out; adhesive eggs are deposited over shallow, submerged vegetation and left to hatch with no parental care; occasionally spawns in fall with very low survival rate.

Average Size: 10–18 in., 1–2 lb.

Fishing Tip: Small crappie imitation lures are deadly for chain pickerel.

Notes: The chain pickerel is the largest of the pickerel and is a respected game fish. It frequents the outside edges of weedbeds and bites readily on minnow-imitating lures. When fished on light tackle or a fly rod, it is a very sporting catch. Pickerel have a tendency to stunt when overcrowded, filling the lake with half-pound "hammer handles." Removing the small ones when caught will help improve the fishing.

Description: back and sides olive-green to yellow-brown; yellowish wavy bars on sides; dark teardrop below eye; fins cream to pale yellow; scales on entire cheek and gill covers

Similar Species: chain pickerel (page 122), northern pike (page 128), redfin pickerel (page 126)

Grass Pickerel

bar under eye

Northern Pike

no bar under eye

Grass Pickerel

lacks distinct chainlike marks

Chain Pickerel

chainlike marks on sides

Grass Pickerel

more than 6 notched scales between pelvic fins

Redfin Pickerel

up to 3 notched scales between pelvic fins

GRASS PICKEREL

Esox americanus vermiculatus

Other Names: mud or little pickerel; grass or mud pike

Habitat: shallow, weedy lakes and sluggish streams

Range: Mississippi and upper Ohio River drainages; eastern Great Lakes drainage; Gulf Coastal Plain from Mississippi to Florida

Food: small fish, aquatic insects, frogs

Reproduction: Spawning takes place in April and May just as the ice goes out; adhesive eggs are deposited over shallow submerged vegetation; eggs are left to hatch with no parental care; similar spawning biology results in occasional hybridization with chain pickerel.

Average Size: 10–12 in., 8–10 oz.

Fishing Tip: Frog-colored poppers work well.

Notes: The grass pickerel and the redfin pickerel are varieties of the same species. The redfin is the Atlantic Coastal variety, while the grass pickerel is the central US variety. Both inhabit dense aquatic vegetation and, though small, are scrappy fighters on light tackle. The relationship between the grass pickerel and the northern pike is unclear. In some lakes, they coexist; other lakes have one species or the other.

Description: back and sides olive-green to yellow-brown; sides have wormlike bars; distinct dark teardrop below eye; lower fins are tinged red, bright red in breeding males; scales on the entire cheek and gill cover

Similar Species: chain pickerel (page 122), grass pickerel (page 124), northern pike (page 128)

Redfin Pickerel

bar under eye

Northern Pike

no bar under eye

Redfin Pickerel

lacks distinct chainlike marks

Chain Pickerel

chainlike marks on sides

Redfin Pickerel

up to 3 notched scales between pelvic fins

Grass Pickerel

more than 6 notched scales between pelvic fins

REDFIN PICKEREL

Esox americanus americanus

Other Names: little or mud pickerel; red, grass, or mud pike

Habitat: shallow, weedy lakes and sluggish streams

Range: Atlantic coastal plain; Gulf slope drainage from about Apalachicola through North Florida

Food: small fish, frogs, and aquatic invertebrates

Reproduction: Spawning takes place in early spring just as the ice goes out, when adults enter flooded meadows and shallow bays to lay eggs in less than 2 feet of water; adhesive eggs are deposited over shallow submerged vegetation; eggs are left to hatch with no parental care; similar spawning biology results in occasional hybridization with chain pickerel.

Average Size: 10–12 in., 6–10 oz.

Fishing Tip: Fish small spinner baits along weedbed edges.

Notes: The grass pickerel and the redfin pickerel are varieties of the same species. The redfin is the Atlantic Coastal variety; the grass pickerel is the central US variety. They comingle in the Gulf states but are separated by range in most states. Both inhabit dense aquatic vegetation and, though small, are scrappy fighters on light tackle. Redfin pickerel eat some small fish, but their diet is mainly larger invertebrates, including crayfish.

Description: long body with dorsal fin near the tail; head long and flattened in front, forming a ducklike snout; dark-green back; light-green sides with bean-shaped light spots; silver pike a rare, silver-colored mutation of northern pike

Similar Species: muskellunge and tiger muskie (page 130)

Northern Pike

light marks on dark background

Muskellunge

dark marks on light background

Northern Pike

5 or fewer pores on each side under the jaw

Muskellunge

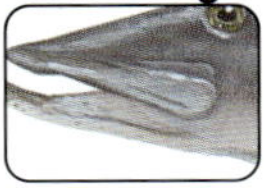

6 or more pores on each side under the jaw

Northern Pike

rounded tail

Muskellunge

pointed tail

Tiger Muskie

rounded tail

NORTHERN PIKE

Esox lucius

Other Names: pickerel, jack, gator, hammerhandle, snot rocket

Habitat: lakes, ponds, streams, and rivers; often found near weeds; small pike tolerate water temperatures up to 70° F, but larger fish prefer cooler water (55° F or lower)

Range: Holarctic across Northern Europe, Asia, and North America; native to north-central and eastern US; now widely introduced in US

Food: small fish, crayfish, and frogs

Reproduction: Late March–early April in tributaries and marshes, when water reaches 34° F–40° F; attended by 1–3 males, female deposits eggs in shallow vegetation.

Average Size: 18–30 in., 1–10 lb.

Fishing Tip: During the first couple of weeks of the fishing season, floating dead sucker minnows near the bottom in weedy shallows is deadly for big pike.

Notes: One of the world's most widespread game fish, northern pike eagerly hit natural and artificial baits and then fight hard when hooked. Good table quality but bony. Its firm, white flesh can acquire a fishy taste if it comes in contact with the fish's outer slime. Daytime ambush feeders, northern pike often lie in wait in weedy cover, capturing prey with a fast lunge. Big fish often break the line at the boat with this same fast lunge.

Description: torpedo-shaped body; dorsal fin near tail; sides typically silver to silver green with dark spots or bars on light background; pointed lobes on tail and paired fins; no scales on lower half of gill cover

Similar Species: northern pike (page 128)

Muskellunge

dark marks on light background

Northern Pike

light marks on dark background

Muskellunge

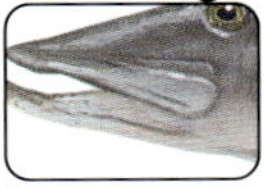

6 or more pores on each side under the jaw

Northern Pike

5 or fewer pores each side under the jaw

Muskellunge

pointed tail

Northern Pike

rounded tail

Tiger Muskie

rounded tail

MUSKELLUNGE/TIGER MUSKIE

Esox masquinongy

Other Names: musky, muskie, ski, lunge

Habitat: large, clear lakes with extensive weedbeds; medium-to-large rivers with slow currents and deep pools

Range: native to upper Mississippi and Ohio River drainages west of the Appalachians and to the Great Lakes drainages; widely introduced in cool-water habitats throughout US

Food: small fish; occasionally muskrats and ducklings

Reproduction: Spawning takes place in mid-April–May when water temperatures reach 50°F–60°F; lays eggs in dead vegetation in tributaries or shallow bays with mucky bottoms; eggs are fertilized and deposited as male and female swim side by side for several hundred yards.

Average Size: 30–40 in., 10–20 lb.

Fishing Tip: Using a bobber, fish with medium-size sucker minnows in open holes in large weedbeds.

Notes: Muskies are legendary among anglers for their sheer size, power, and explosive strikes. They are thinly dispersed (typically 1 fish every 2–3 acres) and noted for being hard to fool with live bait or lures. Studies in Wisconsin have shown that on average it takes 50 hours of fishing to catch a 40-inch fish. Muskies hybridize with northern pike to produce tiger muskies. Because they are less aggressive in rearing tanks, tiger muskies are preferred for stocking programs.

Description: back is dark green to gray-green; sides dark tan with black specks; body has overall purple sheen; dark bar at base of tail; single dorsal fin; big mouth and head; anus just below gills

Similar Species: fathead minnow (page 94)

Pirate Perch

protruding lower jaw

Fathead Minnow

snout protrudes over mouth

Pirate Perch

slight notch in tail

Fathead Minnow

deep notch in tail

PIRATE PERCH

Aphredoderus sayanus

Other Names: green perch

Habitat: low-gradient streams and creeks; ponds, swamps, and roadside ditches, all with soft bottom and thick vegetation

Range: widespread throughout lowlands of Atlantic and Gulf slopes; Mississippi Valley; disjunct population in Lakes Erie and Ontario

Food: small fish, insects, crustaceans

Reproduction: It spawns in early spring through summer; both adults help build nest and then guard eggs and young.

Average Size: 2–5 in.

Fishing Tip: A few anglers feel that this hardy little fish is superior to other baitfish and go to great lengths to obtain it.

Notes: Pirate perch hide in thick vegetation and bottom debris during the day and feed aggressively at night. In juvenile fish, the anus is near the anal fin, but it migrates to the gill area as the fish matures. In other fish, this trait is associated with eggs being brooded under the gill covers, but gill brooding has not been observed in pirate perch. Pirate perch were named for their propensity to attack other fish when kept in aquariums.

Description: blue-gray back; silver-green sides with 5–8 triangular bars of dark gray-brown; deep body; protruding lip; breeding males have blue body with brassy cheeks, breast, and belly and orange fins

Similar Species: mosquitofish (page 76), fathead (page 94)

Sheepshead Minnow

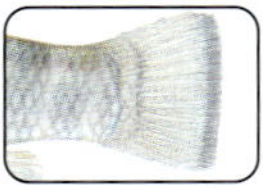

squared tail

Fathead Minnow

deep notch in tail

Mosquitofish

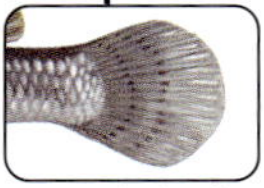

rounded tail

Sheepshead Minnow

rounded anal fin

Mosquitofish

pointed anal fin

SHEEPSHEAD MINNOW

Cyprinodon variegatus

Other Names: chubby, variegated minnow, sheepshead, eustis pupfish

Habitat: quiet shallows of small streams or swamps with a muddy bottom; often found in open water near vegetation; frequents both fresh and brackish waters

Range: Atlantic and Gulf Coastal drainages from Maine to Mexico; parts of the Caribbean

Food: plant material, algae, detritus, aquatic insects

Reproduction: From spring through early summer, males construct and defend nest in open, sandy areas; females lay adhesive eggs that attach to plants or stick to open sand.

Average Size: 2–3 in.

Fishing Tip: This hardy, tough minnow is a prized baitfish for fresh and salt water.

Notes: Pupfish are best-known for being found in desert pools in the West. Most of the desert species are now exceedingly rare. The sheepshead minnow is a very common fish in the central and eastern US, often found in brackish water over much of its range. Sheepshead minnows that inhabit lakes are not as thick-bodied as those found in brackish water and take on a much more elongated shape. This large, stout minnow is a popular aquarium fish and baitfish. Sheepshead minnows are very hardy, even in marine conditions. They are one of the preferred baits for flounder fishing. When introduced to new habitats, sheepshead minnows often outcompete and eliminate native species. They readily hybridize with local pupfish species.

Description: striking iridescent appearance; sail-like dorsal fin is dusky brown to dark gray with rows of red, purple, or bluish spots; dark back; grayish-silver sides with dark spots; pelvic fins marked with pink-to-orange stripes

Similar Species: mountain whitefish (page 164)

Arctic Grayling

spotted, sail-like dorsal fin

Mountain Whitefish

small triangular dorsal fin lacks spots

ARCTIC GRAYLING

Thymallus arcticus

Other Names: bluefish, sailfin

Habitat: clear, cold lakes and rivers; prefers water temperatures at or below 50°F

Range: native to northeastern Asia; central Canada from Hudson Bay to Alaska; upper Missouri River and a few Great Lakes drainages; introduced in some cool, deep US lakes

Food: insects, small fish, crustaceans

Reproduction: Adults spawn over gravel or rock in tributary streams when spring water temperatures reach 44°F–50°F.

Average Size: 12–16 in., 8–16 oz.

Fishing Tip: Fish with small spinner baits or flies with a slow retrieve then a drop.

Notes: The Arctic grayling is one of the most beautiful fish found in North America. Graylings are probably the most iconic and prized trophies for fly anglers. They have mostly been extirpated from the continental US but have been stocked in a few cold lakes, and reportedly there is a native population in the Big Hole River in Montana.

Description: dark-brown-to-olive back; sides lighter, fading to cream belly; sides have light-red or pink spots on a dark background; cream border on pelvic and anal fins; breeding colors range from intense gold to red orange

Similar Species: brook trout (page 150) and kokanee salmon (page 148)

Arctic Char

back lacks wormlike markings

Brook Trout

wormlike markings on back

Arctic Char

anal fin not longer than it is deep

Kokanee Salmon

anal fin longer than it is deep

ARCTIC CHAR

Salvelinus alpinus

Other Names: blueback char, blueback trout

Habitat: deep pools and runs of cold-water rivers; deep, cold, clear areas of lakes with ample oxygen and temperatures between the mid-40s and 50° F

Range: circumpolar; native in Alaska and the Aleutian Islands south to Maine and New Hampshire; stocked in a few deep lakes in the West

Food: crustaceans, insects, plankton, small fish

Reproduction: It typically matures in 2–4 years; spawns over rock or gravel shoals August–October, when water temperatures drop below 50° F; in some lake-run populations, adults gather near inlet streams before moving back into the lake to spawn; thought to spawn in alternate years; does not build nest, or redd.

Average Size: 13–20 in., 1–4 lb.

Fishing Tip: Reportedly, char can be caught through the ice with silver spoons. Inuit traditionally used bone, antler, and shell spoons.

Notes: The Arctic char is found around the world in polar regions and is the most northerly species of freshwater fish. Except for a few stocking programs, Arctic char have been extirpated from the northeastern US. Char come in many shapes and colors and are one of the most variable vertebrates on Earth.

Description: greenish-brown shading on back; silverish-brown sides; light-gray belly; black spots on sides; mouth extends no farther than back of eye

Similar Species: brown trout (page 152)

Atlantic Salmon

mouth extends no farther than back of eye

Brown Trout

mouth extends beyond back of eye

ATLANTIC SALMON

Salmo salar

Other Names: Sebago or Kennebec salmon, ouananiche

Habitat: open ocean and coastal streams; large clear lakes; some native landlocked populations

Range: native to North Atlantic Ocean from Portugal to Arctic Circle and northeastern US south to Delaware; widely introduced

Food: plankton when young, small fish as adults

Reproduction: Both marine and freshwater adults ascend tributary streams in fall to build nests on gravel bars; adults may breed multiple times during their lives; young spend several years in streams before returning to the sea.

Average Size: 16–28 in., 8–10 lb.

Fishing Tip: Keep your fly moving, not giving the salmon long to think about striking or not.

Notes: Historically there were once both landlocked and sea-run Atlantic salmon in the northeastern US. Lake Ontario and the St. Lawrence River were one of the most renowned salmon fisheries in the world. With overfishing, dam building, and pollution, salmon fishing has all but disappeared from the Northeast. Stocking programs in some waters have at least returned Arctic salmon to sportfishing levels.

Description: back and upper sides iridescent green to blue-green; silver below lateral line; small spots on back and tail; inside of mouth is dark; breeding males are olive-brown to purple with pronounced kype (hooked snout)

Similar Species: coho salmon (page 144), pink salmon (page 146), rainbow trout (page 158)

Chinook Salmon

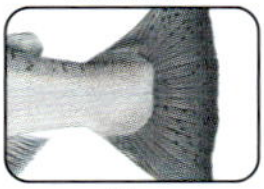

small spots throughout tail

Coho Salmon

spots only on top half of tail

Pink Salmon

eye-size spots throughout tail

Chinook Salmon

inside of mouth is dark

Coho Salmon

inside of mouth is gray

Rainbow Trout

inside of mouth is white

CHINOOK SALMON

Oncorhynchus tshawytscha

Other Names: king salmon, spring salmon, tyee, quinnat, black mouth

Habitat: coastal open ocean; large, clear, gravel-bottomed rivers, and large lakes

Range: native to Pacific Ocean and tributary drainages in Asia, northern Japan, and Russia; in North America from Southern California to Alaska; introduced to the Atlantic Coast in Maine and the Great Lakes

Food: fish, some crustaceans when young

Reproduction: Pacific population ascends coastal rivers to build nests and spawn; Chinooks in the Great Lakes mature in 3–5 years; in October and November, they migrate upstream to attempt nesting on gravel bars; adults die shortly after.

Average Size: 24–30 in., 8–15 lb.

Fishing Tip: Salmon are picky about color. When the bite is slow, keep changing lure color. Chartreuse is always a good bet.

Notes: The largest member of the salmon family, the Chinook may reach 40 lb. in lakes and much more in the Pacific Ocean. Though its population is decreasing, it is still an important commercial and sport fish. Since 1965, a stable population of hatchery-reared fish has been maintained in some of the Great Lakes. Chinooks now reproduce naturally in Lake Superior.

Description: dark metallic-blue-to-green back; silver sides and belly; small dark spots on back, sides, and upper half of tail; inside of mouth is gray; breeding adults have gray-to-green head and red-to-maroon sides; males develop kype (hooked snout)

Similar Species: Chinook salmon (page 142), pink salmon (page 146), rainbow trout (page 158)

Coho Salmon

spots only in top half of tail

Chinook Salmon

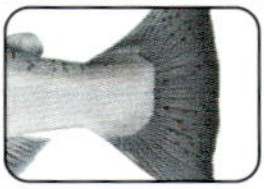

small spots throughout tail

Pink Salmon

eye-size spots throughout tail

Coho Salmon

inside of mouth is gray

Rainbow Trout

inside of mouth is white

COHO SALMON

Oncorhynchus kisutch

Other Names: silver salmon, sea trout, blueback

Habitat: open ocean near clear, gravel-bottomed spawning streams; within 10 miles of shore on the Great Lakes

Range: native to the Pacific Ocean north from California to Japan; introduced into the Great Lakes and a few other large lakes in the northern US

Food: insects, smelt, alewives

Reproduction: Spawning takes place in October and November; adults migrate up tributary streams to build nests on gravel bars; adults die shortly after spawning.

Average Size: 14–20 in., 3–5 lb.

Fishing Tip: In late fall, fishing gold spoons from piers can be productive.

Notes: Coho salmon are very strong fighters and excellent table fare. There are still good populations in some areas along the Pacific Coast, where they support a strong commercial and sport fishery. The coho was stocked in the Great Lakes in 1965 and a few other lakes in the northern US soon after. There is little natural reproduction in most of these lakes, but a few support a reproducing population. Coho salmon are now a popular sport fish in the Great Lakes.

Description: steel-blue-to-blue-green back with silver sides; dark spots on back and tail, some as large as the eye; breeding males develop a large hump in front of the dorsal fin and a hooked upper jaw (kype); both sexes pink during spawning

Similar Species: Chinook salmon (page 142), coho salmon (page 144), brown trout (page 152), rainbow trout (page 158)

Pink Salmon

eye-size spots throughout tail

Chinook Salmon

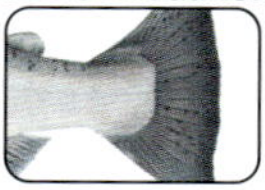

small spots throughout tail

Coho Salmon

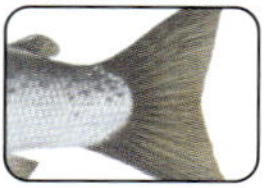

spots only in top half of tail

Pink Salmon

dark tongue and jaw tip

Coho Salmon

inside of mouth is gray

Brown Trout

inside of mouth is white

Rainbow Trout

inside of mouth is white

PINK SALMON

Oncorhynchus gorbuscha

Other Names: humpback salmon, humpy, autumn salmon

Habitat: coastal Pacific Ocean and open water of the Great Lakes; spawns in clear streams

Range: coastal Pacific and Arctic Oceans from Northern California to Alaska and Japan; introduced to Great Lakes

Food: small fish, crustaceans

Reproduction: Spawning takes place in the fall in tributary streams, usually at 2 years of age; female builds nest on gravel bar then covers fertilized eggs; adults die after spawning.

Average Size: Sea run: 15–20 in., 2–4 lb. Landlocked: 12–18 in., 1–2 lb.

Fishing Tip: Fish with small, bright, active lures and flies to entice open-water fish just before spawning.

Notes: The pink salmon is the smallest and most abundant salmon native to North America. This Pacific salmon was unintentionally released into Thunder Bay on Lake Superior in 1956 and has since spread throughout the Great Lakes. It spends 2–3 years in coastal ocean waters or lakes, then moves into streams to spawn and die. Coastal pink salmon sometimes wander and don't return to their birth stream to spawn. Pink salmon only have large spawns every other year. They are not popular with anglers and are not considered great table fare. The flesh deteriorates rapidly, so the fish must be quickly put on ice if they are going to be kept.

Description: greenish-blue back and bluntly pointed head; silver sides and belly; small black specks on back and tail; 13 soft rays in anal fin; adipose fin; juveniles resemble trout; breeding males have bright-green heads, red bodies, and a well-developed kype (hooked snout)

Similar Species: coho salmon (page 144), Chinook salmon (page 142), rainbow trout (page 158)

Sockeye/ Kokanee Salmon

almost toothless; no spots on tail

Coho Salmon

sharp, medium-size teeth; a few spots on tail

Chinook Salmon

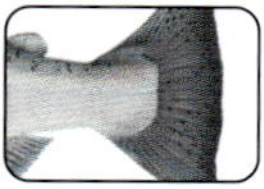

small spots throughout tail

Rainbow Trout

many spots on both lobes of tail

SOCKEYE/KOKANEE SALMON

Oncorhynchus nerka

Other Names: red salmon, silver trout

Habitat: Sockeye: in the open ocean and large, clear, gravel-bottomed spawning rivers. Kokanee: in landlocked lakes and spawning streams.

Range: Sockeye: Pacific Ocean north from California to Canada and west to Japan. Kokanee: coastal lakes in northwest North America; introduced in northeastern US lakes.

Food: zooplankton, crustaceans, aquatic insects

Reproduction: Spawning takes place in the fall, usually in tributary streams; female digs bed (called a redd) in gravel, sand, or rubble; parents guard nest until death.

Average Size: Sockeye: 18–24 in., 4–12 lb. Kokanee: 9–14 in., 8–20 oz.

Fishing Tip: Spawning fish do not feed but can be hooked with bright, shiny lures and flies.

Notes: The kokanee salmon is a naturally landlocked variety of sockeye salmon. They look alike and have very similar reproductive behavior but do not hybridize. Both have a different appearance during spawning. With less food in clear freshwater lakes, the kokanee is a much smaller fish. Both are important commercial and sport fish.

Description: back olive or blue-gray to black with wormlike markings; sides bronze to olive with red spots tinged light brown; lower fins red-orange with white leading edge; tail squared or slightly forked

Similar Species: brown trout (page 152), lake trout (page 160), splake, tiger trout

Brook Trout

wormlike marks, red spots

Brown Trout

large dark spots, small red dots

Rainbow Trout

pink stripe on silver body

Lake Trout

sides lack red spots

Brook Trout

tail square to slightly forked

Lake Trout

tail deeply forked

Splake

tail moderately forked

BROOK TROUT/COASTER/ SALTER/SPLAKE/TIGER TROUT

Salvelinus fontinalis

Other Names: speckled, squaretail, or coaster trout; brookie

Habitat: cool, clear streams and small lakes with sand or gravel bottoms and moderate vegetation; coastal in large lakes and Atlantic Ocean; prefers water temperatures of 50° F–60° F or below

Range: native to eastern North America from Hudson Bay drainages through the Appalachian Mountains; widely introduced in cool streams across the US

Food: insects, small fish, leeches, crustaceans

Reproduction: It spawns in late fall, when water temperatures reach 40° F–49° F; spawning takes place on gravel bars in stream riffles and in lakes where springs aerate eggs; female builds 4- to 12-inch-deep nest in gravel (male may guard it during construction), then buries fertilized eggs.

Average Size: Brook trout (stream): 8–10 in., 8–16 oz. Coaster: 12–20 in., 2–8 lb. Salter: 8–10 in., 6–16 oz.

Fishing Tip: Fish along the shore in the evening or early morning with brown or green poppers. Be very quiet, and don't cast a shadow on the water.

Notes: Brook trout are primarily known as a small-stream fish, but there are two other forms. The larger and much longer-lived coaster, found in the Great Lakes, and the smaller salter, native to coastal drainages from Long Island to Hudson Bay. Brook trout commonly hybridize with other trout. The splake is a cross between brook and lake trout. The tiger trout is a cross between brook and brown trout.

Description: back and sides golden brown to olive; large dark spots on sides, dorsal fin, and sometimes upper lobe of tail; red spots with light halos scattered along sides

Similar Species: rainbow trout (page 158), lake trout (page 160), brook trout (page 150), tiger trout (page 150)

Brown Trout

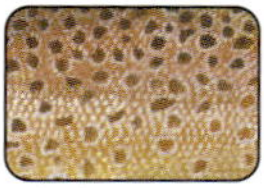

dark spots on brown or olive body

Rainbow Trout

pink stripe on silvery body

Lake Trout

white spots on dark body

Brown Trout

lacks wormlike markings

Brook Trout

wormlike markings on back

Tiger Trout

wormlike markings on back and sides

BROWN TROUT

Salmo trutta

Other Names: German brown, Loch Leven, or spotted trout

Habitat: open ocean near its spawning streams and clear, cold, gravel-bottomed streams; shallow areas of large lakes

Range: native to Europe from the Mediterranean to Arctic Norway and Siberia; widely introduced worldwide

Food: insects, crayfish, small fish

Reproduction: Spawning takes place October–December in stream headwaters and tributaries; stream mouths are used when migration is blocked; female fans out saucer-shaped nest, which male guards until spawning; female covers eggs.

Average Size: 10–20 in., 2–6 lb.

Fishing Tip: A very small spinner tied just ahead of a black-and-gray streamer will sometimes wake up sluggish brown trout.

Notes: This European trout was brought to North America in 1883. A favorite of anglers, it is a secretive, elusive fish that fights hard and has a fine, delicate flavor. It often feeds aggressively on cloudy, rainy days and at night. It tolerates warmer, cloudier water than other trout, allowing it to live in the lower reaches of cold-water streams. Though it can survive in 80°F water for a short time, it prefers the 50s to lower 60s. It hybridizes with brook trout to produce the sterile tiger trout.

Description: blood-red stripes on each side of throat under jaw; round, dark spots on sides and tail; breeding males develop crimson head, side, and belly

Similar Species: brook trout (page 150), rainbow trout (page 158), cutbow

All Cutthroats

red slash mark on throat

Brook Trout

lacks red slash mark on throat

Rainbow Trout

lacks red slash mark on throat

CUTTHROAT TROUT

Oncorhynchus clarkii

Other Names: Clark's, red-throated or mountain trout, cutt, greenback

Habitat: coastal marine waters and freshwater coastal streams; landlocked fish in clear, cool headwater streams and cold lakes

Range: marine cutthroats from central California to Alaska; landlocked varieties from east slope of Rockies west; introduced into some Great Lakes drainages

Food: fish; insects, crustaceans

Reproduction: Marine varieties ascend freshwater streams to spawn; both marine and freshwater varieties build nest in fine gravel in the spring.

Average Size: 12–18 in., 1–3 lb.

Fishing Tip: In streams, fish deep pools with a good vegetation line. In lakes, fish around boulders or rock outcrops.

Notes: The cutthroat trout has the widest native range of all the trout, reaching from the Pacific east to the western drainages of the Mississippi and Missouri Rivers. There are four species of cutthroats and many subspecies that are often hard to separate. Nine states claim them as state fish. Occasionally in nature, cutthroats will hybridize with rainbow trout, producing a fertile hybrid called a cutbow.

Description: brown-to-olive back; golden yellowish sides with crimson stripe and dark markings along lateral line; red gill covers; adipose fin; triangular dorsal fin

Similar Species: rainbow trout (page 158)

Golden Trout

red stripe through large dark spots

Rainbow Trout

pale pink stripe, small spots

Cutthroat

many large dark spots

Golden Trout

white tip on anal, dorsal, and pelvic fins

Cutthroat

lacks white tip on anal, dorsal, and pelvic fins

GOLDEN TROUT

Oncorhynchus aguabonita

Other Names: gold mountain trout

Habitat: clean, clear lakes and streams

Range: native to 2 river systems in California; introduced into several Western states

Food: insects, crustaceans, fish

Reproduction: It spawns in early summer in stream gravel beds; fans out a shallow nest called a redd; no parental care.

Average Size: 10–20 in., 1–3 lb.

Fishing Tip: Because of their bright color, they are highly susceptible to predation and are very wary; sneak up on the stream.

Notes: This state fish of California is considered by many to be the most beautiful trout in the world. A close relative of rainbow trout, it had a very restricted native range but has been widely introduced in high mountain lakes. Because they do not compete well with non-native trout and often hybridize with rainbow trout, pure populations are rare.

Description: blue-green-to-brown head and back; silver lower sides, often with pink-to-rose stripe; sides, back, dorsal fins, and tail covered with small black spots

Similar Species: brown trout (page 152), brook trout (page 150), pink salmon (page 146), Chinook salmon (page 142)

Rainbow Trout

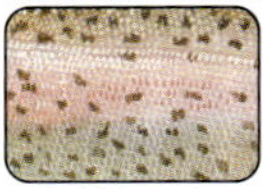

pinkish stripe on silvery body

Brown Trout

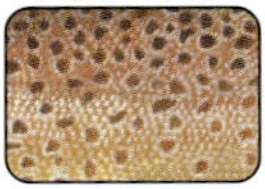

no pinkish stripe

Rainbow Trout

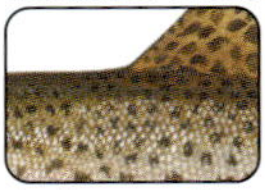

lacks wormlike markings

Brook Trout

wormlike markings on back

Steelhead

white mouth

Pink Salmon

dark tongue and jaw tip

Chinook Salmon

black or dark-gray mouth

RAINBOW TROUT

Oncorhynchus mykiss

Other Names: steelhead, Pacific trout, silver trout, bow

Habitat: coastal marine waters; whitewater in cool streams and coastal regions of large lakes; tolerates smaller cool, clear lakes

Range: Pacific Ocean and coastal streams from Mexico to Alaska and northeast Russia; introduced worldwide

Food: insects, small crustaceans, fish

Reproduction: It's predominantly a spring spawner, but some fall-spawning varieties have been introduced in some states; females build nests in well-aerated gravel in both streams and lakes.

Average Size: 10–20 in., 0.5–6 lb.

Fishing Tip: Small red spinners tipped with a minnow work well in inland lakes stocked with trout.

Notes: This Pacific trout was one of the first North American fish to be widely introduced in other parts of the US and then around the world. Known for acrobatic battles and excellent table quality, it is a renowned sport fish and now widely farmed for food. Both sea-run and lake rainbows that enter streams to spawn are called steelheads. The Kamloops (loopers) is a strain of steelhead trout from British Columbia used in some stocking programs.

Description: dark-gray to gray-green on head, back, top fins, and tail; white spots on sides and unpaired fins; deeply forked tail; inside of mouth is white

Similar Species: brook trout (page 150), splake (page 150)

Lake Trout

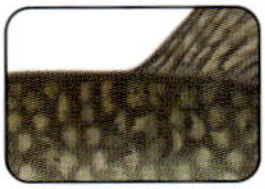

sides lack wormlike markings

Brook Trout

wormlike marks on back

Lake Trout

tail deeply forked

Brook Trout

tail square to slightly forked

Splake

tail moderately forked

LAKE TROUT

Salvelinus namaycush

Other Names: togue, Mackinaw, great gray trout, laker

Habitat: cold (less than 65° F), oxygen-rich waters of deep, clear, infertile lakes

Range: Great Lakes north through Canada; far northeastern US; introduced in a few Western lakes

Food: fish, insects

Reproduction: Females scatter eggs over rocky lake bottoms when the fall water temperatures get below 50° F.

Average Size: 15–20 in., 2–10 lb.

Fishing Tip: In early spring, lake trout can be caught in shallow water along shorelines by floating dead smelt just off the bottom.

Notes: The Great Lakes populations were decimated in the 1950s by overfishing and the sea lamprey. Stocking and lamprey control have restored levels that support sportfishing. In large lakes, lake trout are caught by deep trolling or "surf" fishing mouths of streams. The lake trout hybridizes with the brook trout to produce splake. They may have survived glaciation in refugia in Atlantic Coast and Missouri and upper Mississippi River drainages but not south of the ice sheets in Pacific drainages.

Description: silver with dark-brown-to-olive back and tail; snout protrudes past lower jaw; mouth is small with two small flaps between the openings of each nostril

Similar Species: mooneye (page 104), rainbow smelt (page 170)

Lake Whitefish

adipose fin

Mooneye

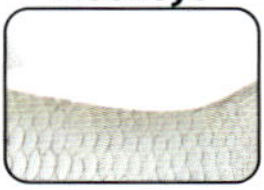

lacks adipose fin

Lake Whitefish

deep body, inconspicuous teeth

Rainbow Smelt

slim body, prominent teeth

LAKE WHITEFISH

Coregonus clupeaformis

Other Names: eastern, common, or Great Lakes whitefish; gizzard fish; Sault whitefish

Habitat: large rivers; large, deep, clean inland lakes with cool, oxygen-rich depths

Range: North America, from Atlantic coastal watersheds across the northern US and Canada

Food: zooplankton, insects, small fish

Reproduction: Whitefish spawn on shallow gravel bars in late fall, when water temperatures reach the low to mid-30s; occasionally ascends streams to spawn.

Average Size: 10–18 in., 1–3 lb.

Fishing Tip: In inland lakes during the warm summer months, lake whitefish can be caught fishing small minnows in the deepest parts of the lake.

Notes: The lake whitefish is a large, abundant cold-water fish of the northern US. It was a significant part of the freshwater commercial fishery until the mid-1950s, when populations began to decline (scientists aren't exactly sure why). They are still commercially harvested from the Great Lakes but in much lower numbers. Just before the ice forms in the fall, lake whitefish enter shallows to spawn; spearing/netting was once a popular fall pastime. A few people still fish or spear whitefish in the winter, and fewer still pull nets under the ice. Along with walleyes, lake whitefish are considered by many to be the finest food fish from Northern waters.

Description: back is dark bluish silver to brown; silver sides; white belly; small head for body size; mouth is under snout; adipose fin; larger scales than trout

Similar Species: Arctic grayling (page 136), kokanee salmon (page 148), lake whitefish (page 162)

Mountain Whitefish

jaw does not extend beyond center of eye

Sockeye/ Kokanee Salmon

jaw extends beyond center of eye

Mountain Whitefish

small triangular dorsal fin lacks spots

Arctic Grayling

sail-like dorsal fin is spotted

Mountain Whitefish

tip of snout below eye

Lake Whitefish

tip of snout above lower edge of eye

MOUNTAIN WHITEFISH

Prosopium williamsoni

Other Names: Rocky Mountain whitefish

Habitat: pools and slow-flowing stretches of midsize-to-large mountain streams; clear, cold lakes and reservoirs; prefers water temperatures below 52° F

Range: native to Hudson Bay and the upper Missouri River drainages

Food: insects, insect larvae, and crustaceans

Reproduction: It matures at 3 years; spawns in streams and along lake shorelines in fall at water temperatures at or below 44° F; small schools form to scatter eggs over gravel or rubble; eggs don't hatch until the following spring.

Average Size: 10–18 in., 1–2 lb.

Fishing Tip: Fish using dry flies near the bottom.

Notes: The mountain whitefish is one of the most common and widespread fish of clear mountain streams in western North America. They are primarily a bottom fish, using the tail and fins to stir bottom sediments to flush out food, mostly at night and at dusk. Mountain whitefish are great fun when feeding on hatching insects near the surface. They are not respected by trout anglers but are strong fighters and taste as good as the trout they target.

Description: blotchy brown coloration; large mouth; eyes set almost on top of broad head; large, winglike pectoral fins; lacks scales

Similar Species: round goby (page 64)

Mottled Sculpin

lacks scales

Round Goby

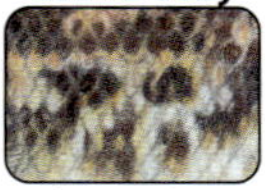

has scales on body

MOTTLED SCULPIN

Cottus bairdii

Other Names: common sculpin, muddler, gudgeon

Habitat: cool, mineral-rich streams and clear lakes; favors areas with rocks or vegetation

Range: scattered, disjunct populations in Savannah, Mobile, and Tennessee River drainages; through the Great Lakes to Hudson Bay; and one in the Rocky Mountains

Food: aquatic invertebrates, fish eggs, small fish

Reproduction: It spawns in April and May in water that's 63° F–74° F; male fans out a cavity beneath a rock ledge or log and then attracts females via vigorous courtship displays; spawning females turn upside down and deposit eggs on underside of nest cover; male guards and cleans the eggs after spawning.

Average Size: 4–5 in.

Fishing Tip: Sculpins could be used for bait but are hard to collect in any numbers.

Notes: There are about 30 species of sculpins in the US; all prefer cool streams or clear Northern lakes. Though scary-looking, they are perfectly harmless and a food source for a variety of predators. Sculpins can modify their body color to blend in with the surroundings. The similar-looking round goby—an invasive Eurasian species that entered the US in the ballast water of oceangoing ships—has been recorded in 10 Northeastern states and should not be used for bait.

Description: long, thin body; sides bright silver with conspicuous black stripe; upturned mouth; two dorsal fins

Similar Species: common shiner (page 98) and rainbow smelt (page 170)

BROOK SILVERSIDE

Labidesthes sicculus

Other Names: northern or brook silverside, skipjack, friar

Habitat: surface of clear lakes and large streams

Range: Mississippi and southern Great Lakes basins; Gulf Coastal Plain from Texas to Florida; Atlantic slope to South Carolina

Food: aquatic and flying insects, spiders

Reproduction: It spawns in late spring and early summer; eggs are laid in sticky strings that attach to vegetation; adults die soon after spawning.

Average Size: 2–4 in.

Fishing Tip: Silversides are not well suited to use as bait. They are not hardy and tend to jump out of the bait pail.

Notes: The brook silverside belongs to a large family of fish that is mostly tropical or subtropical and primarily found in salt water. It is a flashy fish often seen cruising near the surface in small schools. Its upturned mouth is an adaptation for surface feeding. It is not uncommon to see a brook silverside leap from the water, flying fish–style, in pursuit of prey. Because of this tendency to jump, coupled with a lack of hardiness when kept in captivity, it is a poor aquarium fish, despite its beauty.

Description: large mouth with prominent teeth; jaw extends to rear margin of eye; dark-green back; violet-blue sides and white belly; deeply forked tail; adipose fin

Similar Species: lake whitefish (page 162), common shiner (page 98), brook silverside (page 168)

Rainbow Smelt

adipose fin

Common Shiner

lacks adipose fin

Brook Silverside

lacks adipose fin

Rainbow Smelt

slim profile, prominent teeth

Whitefish

deep profile, inconspicuous teeth

RAINBOW SMELT

Osmerus mordax

Other Names: ice or frost fish, lake herring, leefish

Habitat: open oceans and large lakes; tributaries at spawning

Range: coastal Pacific, Atlantic, and Arctic Oceans; landlocked in northeastern US and southeastern Canada

Food: crustaceans, insect larvae, small fish

Reproduction: Spawning takes place in May, at night, in the first mile of tributary streams.

Average Size: 5–10 in.

Fishing Tip: Smelt are good lake trout bait; fish them near the bottom in early spring.

Notes: A saltwater fish that enters freshwater to spawn, the rainbow smelt was introduced in some of the Great Lakes in 1912 to support salmon stocks. This small fish flourished and was soon making spectacular spawning runs in some Great Lakes streams. With the introduction of salmon and the recovery of lake trout, the smelt population crashed in the 1980s and has not fully recovered.

Description: dark-brown back fading to lighter-brown sides; long dorsal and anal fins; large scales on head; large mouth with sharp teeth. Northern: irregular blotches on sides. Bullseye: dark spots on sides.

Similar Species: American eel (page 54), bowfin (page 28), burbot (page 50)

Snakeheads

enlarged scales on head; no barbels

American Eel

no head scales; bony plates between jaws

Burbot

barbel on chin

Snakeheads

long anal fin not fused to tail

American Eel

anal fin fused to tail

Bowfin

short anal fin

NORTHERN SNAKEHEAD *Channa argus*
BULLSEYE SNAKEHEAD *Channa marulius*

Other Names: Amur, ocellated, spotted, or cobra snakehead; Frankenfish

Habitat: stagnant, shallow ponds and slow-moving streams with muddy and weedy bottom

Range: native to Asia and Eastern Europe; introduced in US. Northern snakehead: northern Atlantic coastal plain. Bullseye snakehead: Florida; expanding range along the Gulf.

Food: fish, crayfish, frogs

Reproduction: Females can spawn several times a year beginning in June; females can lay 100,000 eggs.

Average Size: 12–24 in., 2–5 lb.

Fishing Tip: Fishing bass lures with a fast retrieve along weed lines works well.

Notes: Northern snakeheads and bullseye snakeheads (Gulf states) were brought to the US for the live fish markets and as aquarium pets, then escaped or were released. Snakeheads are farmed for food in Asia. Both have a modified swim bladder that allows them to breathe air; they can slither through wet marshes for up to 3 days to reach new lakes. Northern snakeheads can tolerate temperatures from freezing to near 90°F. The bullseye snakehead is now found only in the warm waters of the Gulf but can survive in much cooler water. These highly competitive invaders have the potential to devastate native fish populations. Anglers should learn to identify snakeheads, and any that are caught should be killed.

BROOK STICKLEBACK

NINESPINE STICKLEBACK

Description: Both brook and ninespine sticklebacks are brown with torpedo-shaped bodies and a very narrow caudal peduncle (the area just before the tail); front portion of dorsal fin has short separated spines; pelvic fins are abdominal and reduced to a single spine; small, sharp teeth.

Similar Species: ninespine stickleback

Brook Stickleback

4–6 dorsal spines (usually 5)

Ninespine Stickleback

8–11 dorsal spines (usually 9)

BROOK STICKLEBACK *Culaea inconstans*
NINESPINE STICKLEBACK *Pungitius pungitius*

Other Names: common stickleback, spiny minnow

Habitat: shallows of cool streams and lakes

Range: Brook: northern Mississippi and Ohio River drainages, northeast through Canada. Ninespine: native range is circumpolar; north-central and eastern US.

Food: small aquatic animals; occasionally algae

Reproduction: When water reaches 50°F–68°F, the male builds a golf ball–size globular nest of sticks, algae, and other plant matter on submerged vegetation; females deposit eggs and depart, often plowing a hole in the side of the nest in the process; the male repairs any damage and viciously guards the eggs until they hatch; an ambitious male may build a second, larger nest and transfer the eggs.

Average Size: 1–3 in.

Fishing Tip: Sticklebacks are often found mixed in with crappie minnows and are discarded by anglers, but they are fine as bait.

Notes: Most members of the stickleback family are marine fish. Some are equally at home in fresh or salt water, and a few are strictly freshwater varieties. The brook stickleback is the most common stickleback in the US and can be found in most streams and lakes in the north-central states. The ninespine stickleback is less common but has populations scattered across the north-central US. These pugnacious little predators make fun aquarium fish and will readily build and defend nests in captivity.

Description: dark-brown back and sides; brown fins; bony plates on skin; tail lacks plates and is sharklike, with upper lobe longer than lower; blunt snout with four barbels; spiracles (openings between eye and corner of gill)

Similar Species: shovelnose sturgeon (page 178)

Lake Sturgeon

spiracle between eye and gill

Shovelnose Sturgeon

lacks spiracles

LAKE STURGEON

Acipenser fulvescens

Other Names: rock sturgeon, smoothback

Habitat: deep, quiet waters of large rivers and lakes

Range: Mississippi, Missouri, and Red River (Minnesota) drainages west of the Appalachians, south to Alabama, north to Hudson Bay

Food: snails, clams, crayfish, aquatic insects

Reproduction: It spawns April–June in lake shallows and tributary streams; a single female may produce up to 1 million eggs.

Average Size: 20–40 in., 10–30 lb.

Fishing Tip: Large crayfish tails are good sturgeon bait.

Notes: Lake and white sturgeons are North America's largest freshwater fish. Lake sturgeons historically often reached weights in excess of 100 lb. and could live for 100 years. Today, due to commercial fishing, dams, habitat alteration, and pollution, this slow-growing fish averages 5–40 lb. and is relatively rare except in select waters. Thanks to a regulated harvest, cleaner water, and improved access to habitat, sturgeon are slowly increasing in numbers in some areas.

Description: coppery, dark-tan or light-brown back and sides; light belly; long, flat snout; shovel-shaped head; bony plates instead of scales; sharklike tail with upper lobe ending in a long filament

Similar Species: lake sturgeon (page 176)

Shovelnose Sturgeon

lacks spiracles

Lake Sturgeon

spiracle between eye and gill

SHOVELNOSE STURGEON

Scaphirhynchus platorynchus

Other Names: hackleback, sand sturgeon, switchtail

Habitat: open, flowing channels of rivers and large streams, typically with sand or gravel bottom

Range: Missouri, Mississippi, and Ohio River drainages west of Appalachian Mountains; formerly Rio Grande

Food: clams, snails, crayfish, aquatic insects

Reproduction: Spawning takes place in May and June in water temperatures of 65° F–71° F; adults migrate upriver or into small tributaries to spawn over gravel or rocks in swift current.

Average Size: 18–24 in., 2–3 lb.

Fishing Tip: Fish worms or crayfish tails on the bottom in deep channels.

Notes: The shovelnose sturgeon is the smallest sturgeon in North America. The prehistoric-looking family to which it belongs has cartilage instead of bones and hard plates in place of scales. Like the other sturgeons, it suctions food off the bottom. Once netted commercially for both meat and caviar, it is now uncommon in most waters due largely to a loss of spawning and nursery habitat.

Description: gray back and sides; gray fins; shovel-shaped head; chin barbels closer to snout than mouth; bony plates (scuts) instead of scales; sharklike tail

Similar Species: lake sturgeon (page 176)

White Sturgeon

barbels closer to snout tip than mouth

Lake Sturgeon

barbels closer to mouth than snout tip

WHITE STURGEON

Acipenser transmotanus

Other Names: sea or ocean sturgeon

Habitat: found in shallow coastal waters and estuaries; large tributary streams

Range: Pacific slope of North America, landlocked in upper Columbia River and Lake Shasta, California; introduced in lower Colorado River

Food: fish, clams, squid

Reproduction: Females mature at 10 to 20 years, then spawn every 2 to 4 years over gravel bars in coastal tributary streams.

Average Size: 3–5 ft., 30–200 lb.

Fishing Tip: Fish using dead whole bait fish in deep, soft-bottom pools of coastal estuaries.

Notes: The white sturgeon is the largest freshwater fish in North America, historically reaching over 1,000 lb. Once spawning from Mexico to the Aleutian Islands, their numbers have been greatly reduced by overharvesting for caviar. There are landlocked populations in the upper Columbia River and Lake Shasta in California that may have been isolated for thousands of years.

Description: olive-brown-to-bronze back; sides dull olive fading to white belly; blunt snout; rounded head; long dorsal fin; upper lip even with lower margin of eye

Similar Species: common carp (page 82), black buffalo (page 184), smallmouth buffalo (page 186)

Bigmouth Buffalo

upper lip level with lower edge of eye

Black Buffalo

upper lip well below eye

Smallmouth Buffalo

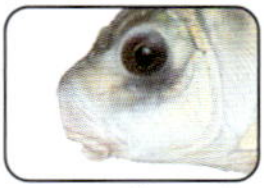

upper lip well below eye

Bigmouth Buffalo

forward-facing mouth, lacks barbels

Common Carp

downturned mouth with barbels

BIGMOUTH BUFFALO

Ictiobus cyprinellus

Other Names: baldpate, blue router, mongrel, round buffalo

Habitat: soft-bottomed shallows of large lakes, sloughs, and oxbows; slow-flowing streams and rivers

Range: Missouri, Mississippi, Ohio, and Red River (Minnesota) drainages; Lake Erie drainage

Food: small mollusks, insect larvae, zooplankton

Reproduction: It makes spectacular spawning runs in clear, shallow water of flooded fields and marshes during April and May; spawns when water temperatures reach the low 60s.

Average Size: 18–24 in., 10–15 lb.

Fishing Tip: Buffalo are filter feeders that are hard to hook but can be caught by floating small pieces of nightcrawlers in slow backwater currents.

Notes: The bigmouth buffalo is a schooling, big-water fish that inhabits large, shallow lakes and sluggish streams and large rivers. They are slow-growing fish that may live over 70 years. This large sucker can withstand low oxygen levels, high water temperatures, and some turbidity but prefers clear, clean water for foraging.

Description: back is slate-green to dark gray; sides have a blue-bronze sheen; deep body with a sloping back that supports a long dorsal fin; upper lip well below eye

Similar Species: bigmouth buffalo (page 182), smallmouth buffalo (page 186), common carp (page 82)

Black Buffalo

upper lip well below eye

Bigmouth Buffalo

upper lip level with lower edge of eye

Smallmouth Buffalo

upper lip well below eye

Black Buffalo

mouth lacks barbels

Common Carp

barbels below mouth

BLACK BUFFALO

Ictiobus niger

Other Names: buoy tender; current or deepwater buffalo

Habitat: deep, fast water of large streams; deep sloughs, backwaters, and impoundments

Range: Missouri, Mississippi, and Ohio River basins

Food: aquatic insects, crustaceans, algae

Reproduction: Spawning takes place in April and May; fish move up tributaries to lay eggs in flooded sloughs and marshes.

Average Size: 15–20 in., 8–10 lb.

Fishing Tip: Fish the mouth of tributary streams with small baits during the spawning run.

Notes: The black buffalo is a Southern species that is uncommon but present in the Missouri and upper Mississippi Rivers. It inhabits the deep, strong currents of large rivers, hence the nickname "current buffalo." It is rarely caught on hook and line but is notable because of its size and strong fight. Black buffalo can hybridize with smallmouth buffalo.

Description: slate-green back with bronze sides; large, dark eye; deep, laterally compressed body; rounded head; blunt snout; small, downturned mouth with thick lips

Similar Species: common carp (page 82), bigmouth buffalo (page 182), black buffalo (page 184)

Smallmouth Buffalo

upper lip well below eye

Bigmouth Buffalo

upper lip level with eye

Smallmouth Buffalo

mouth lacks barbels

Common Carp

barbels below mouth

Smallmouth Buffalo

back steeply arched with pronounced hump

Black Buffalo

rounded back without hump

SMALLMOUTH BUFFALO

Ictiobus bubalus

Other Names: razorback, highback, humpback, or thick-lipped buffalo

Habitat: moderate to swift currents in the deep, clean water of larger streams and lakes

Range: Missouri, Mississippi, Ohio River, and Gulf slope drainages; Rio Grande basin; introduced in Arizona

Food: insect larvae, small crustaceans

Reproduction: Spawning takes place in flooded fields and marshes in early summer, when water temperatures reach the low 60s.

Average Size: 15–24 in., 5–10 lb.

Fishing Tip: Drift small, prepared baits or insects in the mouth of tributary streams.

Notes: Smallmouth buffalo are big fish that prefer deeper, cleaner water and feed more heavily on aquatic insect larvae than the other buffalo. Smallmouth buffalo are commercially harvested from larger rivers and impoundments. Some are smoked near their source, but many are shipped live to urban markets.

Description: olive-brown back; silver sides; fins clear; deep body with round blunt head; high, concave dorsal fin; leading edge of dorsal fin higher than base

Similar Species: common carp (page 82), quillback (page 190)

Carpsuckers/ Quillback

no mouth barbels

Common Carp

mouth barbels

River Carpsucker

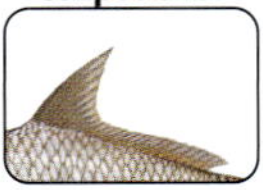

no quill

Highfin Carpsucker

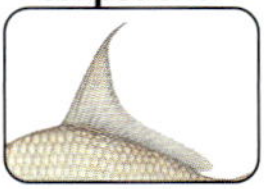

quill longer than base of dorsal fin

Quillback

quill shorter than base of dorsal fin

HIGHFIN CARPSUCKER *Carpiodes velifer*
RIVER CARPSUCKER *Carpiodes carpio*

Other Names: white or silver carp, northern carpsucker

Habitat: quiet silt-bottom pools with low-to-moderate gradients and impoundments

Range: Mississippi River basin from Pennsylvania to Montana; Gulf slope drainage from Mississippi west to the Rio Grande

Food: aquatic insects, small crustaceans, plant debris

Reproduction: It spawns in late spring to early summer over an extended period; adhesive eggs are spread over moderate vegetation or debris; eggs are left without parental care.

Average Size: 11–15 in., 1–2 lb.

Fishing Tip: Carpsuckers can be caught on flies fished along the bottom just outside of any cover.

Notes: There are two carpsuckers in the US, highfin and river. The river carpsucker is the most common. They prefer moderate cover away from the current or nearby shorelines. The two types look much alike, but the highfin has a much taller and more pointed dorsal fin. Carpsuckers are slow, inactive fish that feed during the day and when hooked put up a good fight. Some impoundments can have a relatively high number of carpsuckers that are not often fished for. Both carpsuckers are good smoked.

Description: bright-silver back and sides, often with yellow tinge; fins clear; deep body with round, blunt head; leading edge of dorsal fin extends into a large, arching "quill"

Similar Species: common carp (page 82), smallmouth buffalo (page 186)

Carpsuckers/ Quillback

no mouth barbels

Common Carp

mouth barbels

Quillback

quill slightly shorter than base of dorsal fin

Carpsuckers

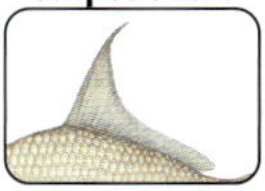

quill much longer than base of dorsal fin

Buffalos

short dorsal fin, no quill

QUILLBACK

Carpiodes cyprinus

Other Names: silver carp, carpsucker, lake quillback

Habitat: slow-flowing streams and rivers; backwaters and lakes, prefers areas with soft bottoms

Range: Mississippi River and major Atlantic slope drainages; Gulf slope drainage into Mobile Bay; Apalachicola (FL) River drainage; south-central Canada through the Great Lakes

Food: insects, plant matter, decaying material on bottom

Reproduction: Spawning takes place in late spring through early summer in tributary streams or lake shallows; eggs are deposited in open areas over sand or mud.

Average Size: 12–14 in., 1–2 lb.

Fishing Tip: In clear streams, drift small pieces of night crawlers into the pools below riffles.

Notes: The quillback is closely related to the two North American carpsuckers, the highfin and river. They all occupy similar ranges and have similar life histories. Quillbacks have a wide range, from the Gulf well into Canada. They are a bottom-feeding, schooling fish with little importance to anglers now, but historically quillbacks were part of the commercial harvest from large lakes and rivers throughout the central US. Quillbacks are hard fighters on light tackle and have firm, white flesh.

Description: back is brassy green to gold; sides bronze to golden green; lower fin yellowish red to dull red; sucker mouth; scale on back and sides with dark spot at base

Similar Species: white sucker (page 202), northern hog sucker (page 200)

Redhorses

lower fins and tail red or orange

Suckers

light-colored lower fins and tail

Redhorses

head rounded between eyes

Suckers

head concave between eyes

GOLDEN REDHORSE

Moxostoma erythrurum

Other Names: golden or smallheaded mullet, golden sucker

Habitat: clean streams and rivers with hard bottoms; rarely, clear lakes with strong tributary streams

Range: Mississippi, Ohio, and lower Missouri River basins; Mobile Bay drainage; lower Great Lakes except Lake Superior drainages; Red River (MN) drainage

Food: aquatic insects, small crustaceans, and plant debris

Reproduction: Spawning takes place in tributary streams in early spring when water temperature reaches the low 60s; males build nest and court with much flourish.

Average Size: 12–20 in., 2–5 lb.

Fishing Tip: Fish using worms or dry flies near the bottom in shallow rapids just above deeper pools.

Notes: There are about a dozen suckers that are called redhorses in the US. All redhorses have sucker mouths and are similar in appearance. The golden is one of the larger and more widespread of the redhorses. The golden redhorse can tolerate warmer water and more turbidity than most of the other redhorses, but all require relatively clean water. Redhorses are not of sporting importance but are a fairly common catch of river fishers. They fight well on light tackle and, though bony, have a good flavor when smoked.

Description: back and sides blue to blue-gray; blue to white below; small, pointed head with a bulbous snout that overhangs its small mouth; sickle-shaped dorsal fin; deeply forked tail

Similar Species: carpsuckers (page 188), quillback (page 190)

Carpsuckers/ Quillback | **Blue Sucker**

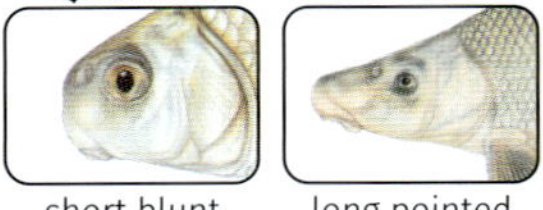

short blunt nose | long pointed nose

BLUE SUCKER

Cycleptus elongatus

Other Names: Missouri, slenderheaded, gourdseed, razorback, or sweet sucker

Habitat: deep chutes with strong currents and gravel bottoms in large rivers; deep river impoundments

Range: Gulf slope drainage from the Rio Grande in Mexico to Mobile Bay; Mississippi, Ohio, and Missouri River drainages

Food: crustaceans, aquatic insects, some plant material

Reproduction: Little is known; spring spawning runs over gravel bars in tributary streams have been noted.

Average Size: 12–18 in., 1–3 lb.

Fishing Tip: Fish on the bottom of deep pools with a strong current running through them.

Notes: The blue sucker is a big-water fish that prefers deep, fast water over a clean gravel bottom. Construction of dams and increasing silt from agricultural fields have reduced the amount of suitable habitat for blue suckers, and their numbers have been declining for years. There is some indication the population is rebounding, thanks to improving conditions in the Mississippi River. It is reported that the blue sucker is a fine food fish and the best-tasting of all the sucker species. A limited number of blue suckers are commercially harvested and sold along the Mississippi River.

Description: black to dark-olive back; slate-gray sides fading to creamy belly; long snout protrudes beyond upper lip

Similar Species: northern hog sucker (page 200), redhorses (page 192), white sucker (page 202)

Longnose Sucker

snout protrudes beyond mouth

White Sucker

snout does not protrude beyond mouth

Northern Hog Sucker

mouth protrudes from snout

LONGNOSE SUCKER

Catostomus catostomus

Other Names: sturgeon, red or redside sucker

Habitat: deep waters of large, cold, clear lakes and occasionally deep pools of clear streams

Range: Great Lakes region through the Northeastern states; upper Missouri and Columbia Rivers and Rocky Mountains; scattered across Canada and Siberia

Food: small crustaceans, plant material

Reproduction: It spawns during daylight in May and June; adults crowd into fast-flowing tributary streams to deposit eggs over gravel bars; fry move into lakes soon after hatching.

Average Size: 15–20 in., 1–2 lb.

Fishing Tip: Drift yellow trout PowerBait among the rocks in river eddies.

Notes: This is a Northern cold-water fish that is found in both the Old and New World. The most widespread sucker in the North, it is found in relatively high numbers in most clear, cold waters. Though primarily known as a shallow-water fish, it has been taken as deep as 600 feet in Lake Superior. Large numbers of longnose suckers crowd some streams during the spring spawning run, making them easy to catch. The longnose sucker is delicious when smoked; in fact, many smoked-fish connoisseurs argue that it is superior to all other suckers in flavor.

Description: stout body; back and sides olive to dark gray or brownish with black dots; sometimes mottling across back; underside white; breeding adults develop red-orange band along sides; dark band on nonbreeding adults

Similar Species: white sucker (page 202) and longnose sucker (page 196)

MOUNTAIN SUCKER

Catostomus platyrhynchus

Other Names: northern or plains mountain sucker

Habitat: riffle areas of clear, cold mountain streams with rock, gravel, or sand bottom; occasionally occurs in turbid (cloudy) streams; rarely found in lakes

Range: mountains of western North America; upper reaches of Missouri River; east into Black Hills of North Dakota; as small population in upper Maine

Food: algae and other plant matter, invertebrates

Reproduction: It matures at 2–5 years; scatters sticky eggs over gravel riffles in early to midsummer when the water temperature passes 50°F; eggs hatch in 8–14 days.

Average Size: 6–10 in., 8–12 oz.

Fishing Tip: Mountain suckers do take flies but are not much of a catch.

Notes: The mountain sucker is a small sucker averaging about 8 in. in length. The breeding males are among the most brightly colored suckers. They are mostly stream fish, but there are a few lake populations. Their distribution ranges from the high Western plains up to 9,000 feet in mountain streams. As in some other suckers, the young have a mouth at the end of their nose, making them look like minnows. The mouth migrates to under the head as the fish matures.

Description: back olive-brown, fading to yellow-brown on sides; 4 or 5 irregular dark saddles; elongated body almost round in cross-section; large head that is concave between the eyes; lower fins light brown

Similar Species: redhorses (page 192), suckers (pages 194–203)

Northern Hog Sucker

lower fins light brown

Redhorses

lower fins red or orange

Suckers

lower fins gray

Northern Hog Sucker

head concave between eyes

Redhorses

head flat between eyes

Suckers

head rounded between eyes

NORTHERN HOG SUCKER

Hypentelium nigricans

Other Names: hog molly, hammerhead, riffle or bighead sucker, crawl-a-bottom

Habitat: riffles and tailwaters of clear streams with hard bottom; a few lakes near mouth of tributary streams

Range: Missouri, Mississippi, and Ohio River basins; Great Lakes drainages; upper reaches of Atlantic slope drainages south to Georgia; recently in Mobile Bay drainage

Food: small crustaceans and aquatic insects

Reproduction: Spawning takes place in spring, when water reaches 60° F; males gather in riffles or shallow pools, where females shed eggs that are fertilized by several males.

Average Size: 8–14 in., 8–20 oz.

Fishing Tip: Fish with worms in riffles near still pools.

Notes: Northern hog suckers are clean-water fish well adapted to feeding in moving water. They use their elongated body and concave head to hold their place in riffles while turning over stones to release food. It is common for other fish to follow hog suckers, feeding on what is stirred up. Hog suckers are not of much interest to anglers but are often caught by fly-fishers working the edges of fast water.

Description: olive-to-brown back; gray-to-silver sides; white belly; gray dorsal fin and tail; other fins clear or whitish; rounded head; blunt snout

Similar Species: longnose sucker (page 196)

White Sucker

snout barely extends past upper lip

Longnose Sucker

snout extends well beyond upper lip

WHITE SUCKER

Catostomus commersonii

Other Names: common, coarse-scaled, or eastern sucker; black mullet

Habitat: occupies wide range of habitats but prefers clean lakes and streams with some rock or gravel areas for spawning

Range: widespread from Arctic Circle south through Canada and central and eastern US to a line from New Mexico to South Carolina; absent from Pacific drainages

Food: insects, crustaceans, plant matter

Reproduction: Spawning takes place over gravel or coarse sand in April and early May; adults migrate up small tributaries; in large lakes, spawning may occur along shoreline shallows.

Average Size: 12–18 in., 1–3 lb.

Fishing Tip: In early spring, fishing with worms at the mouth of small streams can be very productive.

Notes: The white sucker is one of the most common and widespread fish in North America and one of the most important for anglers. Highly productive, it provides a large source of forage for game fish and is a mainstay in the live bait industry. A few fishers pursue white suckers during the spring spawning run with spears or dip nets. White sucker meat is bony but delectable when smoked or used in soups and chowders.

Description: dark-green back; greenish sides, often with dark lateral band; white-to-gray belly; large, forward-facing mouth; lower jaw extends to rear margin of eye

Similar Species: smallmouth bass (page 206)

Largemouth Bass

mouth extends beyond dark-orange eye

Smallmouth Bass

mouth does not extend beyond red eye

LARGEMOUTH BASS

Micropterus salmoides

Other Names: black bass, green bass, green trout, slough bass, bucket mouth

Habitat: shallow, fertile, weedy lakes and river backwaters

Range: native range from northern Mexico to Florida, north in the Mississippi and Ohio River drainages to the Great Lakes; introduced throughout the world

Food: small fish, frogs, crayfish, insects, leeches

Reproduction: In spring, when water temperatures reach 60° F, male builds nest in 2–8 feet of water, usually on firm bottom with weedy cover; male guards eggs and fry until the "brood swarm" disperses.

Average Size: 10–20 in., 1–3 lb.

Fishing Tip: Retrieving lures very slowly is often the most productive approach for bass.

Notes: With spirited battles and acrobatic leaps, largemouth bass are one of the most sought-after freshwater game fish in North America and now the world. World-record fish have been reported from Japan. The largemouth bass is one of the largest members of the sunfish family and will readily devour any live prey or lure that fits in its mouth, making it the ideal target for anglers.

Description: back and sides mottled dark green to bronze or pale gold, often with dark vertical bands; white belly; stout body; large, forward-facing mouth; red eye

Similar Species: largemouth bass (page 204)

Smallmouth Bass

mouth does not extend beyond red eye

Largemouth Bass

mouth extends beyond dark-orange eye

SMALLMOUTH BASS

Micropterus dolomieu

Other Names: bronzeback, brown, or redeye bass; redeye, white, or mountain trout

Habitat: clear, swift-flowing streams and rivers; clear lakes with gravel or rocky shorelines

Range: native to upper Mississippi and Ohio River basins from Great Lakes to Tennessee River system; widely introduced throughout US

Food: small fish, crayfish, insects, frogs

Reproduction: Smallmouths spawn in spring when water temperatures reach mid- to high 60s; males sweep out nest in a gravel bed, typically in 3–10 feet of water; nest is often next to a log or boulder; male guards nest and young until fry disperse.

Average Size: 10–20 in., 1–3 lb.

Fishing Tip: Fish using imitation-crayfish lures in the shade of large rocks or brush.

Notes: Revered by anglers as a world-class game fish, the smallmouth bass is noted for powerful fights and wild jumps. Avoiding weedbeds, it prefers deeper, cooler, and more open water than the largemouth bass. Though the range of this slow-maturing fish has expanded by introduction, its numbers are decreasing in some areas due to overfishing and habitat loss. This hard-fighting fish is considered by many anglers as the epitome of freshwater game fish.

Description: green-to-black back; green-brown sides with dark bars; dark spot on gill; red eye; dark stripes; lower jaw extends to eye; shallow notch between dorsal fins; scales on base of dorsal and anal fins

Similar Species: largemouth bass (page 204), spotted bass (page 212), shoal bass (page 210)

Redeye Bass

red eye

Smallmouth Bass

yellow-red eye

Spotted Bass

yellow eye

Redeye Bass

notched dorsals with scales at base

Largemouth Bass

notched dorsals with no scales at base

REDEYE BASS

Micropterus coosae

Other Names: Flint River bass

Habitat: rocky shallows in rivers and small streams

Range: native to the Chattahoochee, Coosa, and Savannah River systems in Georgia and Alabama; introduced in California and Puerto Rico

Food: small fish, frogs, insects, crayfish

Reproduction: It migrates up small tributary streams to spawn when water temperature reaches 60° F; males build nest, then guard the nest and fry; does not reproduce well in waters without a current.

Average Size: 10–12 in., 12–20 oz.

Fishing Tip: Float green poppers, working across the current.

Notes: The redeye bass is a small bass averaging about 1 lb. with a very restricted range. Redeyes are similar in appearance and habits to smallmouth bass but can be quickly distinguished by the reddish-orange fins. Redeye bass may be found in a few lakes and reservoirs but prefer small tributary streams and can only reproduce where there is a current. Due to their small size and rarity, they are not popular among bass fishers but do have a small and loyal following with some fly-fishers.

Description: dark-green back; greenish sides with dark blotches; dark spot on gill and base of tail; red eye; dark stripes extend from eye; lower jaw extends to front of eye; shallow notch between dorsal fins with scales at their base; no red on caudal fin; 18–19 scale rows below the lateral line and 72–77 scales in the lateral line

Similar Species: largemouth bass (page 204), redeye bass (page 208), spotted bass (page 212)

Shoal/Redeye Bass

mouth does not extend past eye

Largemouth Bass

mouth extends well beyond eye

Shoal Bass

no white on caudal fin

Redeye Bass

white edge on top and bottom of caudal fin

SHOAL BASS

Micropterus cataractae

Other Names: Flint River or Chipola bass

Habitat: rocky shallows in rivers and small streams

Range: Florida Panhandle and southern Georgia; Apalachicola, Chipola, Chattahoochee, and Flint River drainages

Food: small fish, frogs, insects, crayfish

Reproduction: It ascends small tributary streams to spawn when water temperatures reach 60°F; males build nest, then guard the nest and fry.

Average Size: 10–18 in., 1–3 lb.

Fishing Tip: Drift small plastic worms out of rapids into still pools.

Notes: For a long time, shoal bass were considered to be a subspecies of the redeye bass; there is still a great deal of confusion concerning the two, and the records reflect this confusion. In the late 1990s, shoal bass were designated as a separate species. It is now thought that the shoal bass is the predominant fast-water river bass in some streams near the Georgia–Florida line. The surest way to differentiate between the two species is by counting scales. Shoal bass have 18–19 scale rows below the lateral line and 72–77 scales in the lateral line. Redeye bass have 16–17 scale rows below the lateral line and 67–72 scales in the lateral line.

Description: dark-green back with light-green sides; side blotches form a dark stripe, with dark spots above; light spots on each scale below; dark lines extend from red eye

Similar Species: redeye bass (page 208) and smallmouth bass (page 206)

Spotted Bass

no scales on base of tail/anal fin; spot at base of tail

Redeye Bass

scales on base of tail/anal fin; no spot at base of tail

Smallmouth Bass

scales on base of tail/anal fin; no spot at base of tail

Spotted Bass

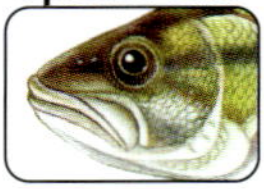

yellow eye

Redeye Bass

red eye

SPOTTED BASS

Micropterus punctulatus

Other Names: Kentucky, speckled, or yellow bass, spottys

Habitat: deep, silted pools in sluggish, medium-to-large streams; larger lakes and reservoirs

Range: lower Mississippi and Ohio River drainages; Gulf slope coastal drainage from Texas to Florida Panhandle

Food: small fish, frogs, crayfish

Reproduction: When water temperatures reach the mid- to high 60s in May and June, males build a nest in open gravel beds in 3–4 feet of water; male aggressively guards the nest and young.

Average Size: 8–18 in., 8 oz.–2 lb.

Fishing Tip: Floating big grasshoppers on the surface is deadly for spotted bass.

Notes: This bass is primarily a stream fish but has done well in impoundments. It is rarely found in natural lakes. In rivers, spotted and shoal bass seek out the rapids, while largemouth bass prefer the edge of weedbeds and deeper pools. In reservoirs, spotted bass like deeper water than largemouth bass, often near the bottom on the outside edge of deep weedbeds or rock ledges. Some anglers feel that spotted bass taste better than largemouth bass.

Description: dark-green back; greenish-brown sides with dark blotches; turquoise lower sides and pectoral fins; red eye; lower jaw extends to eye; shallow notch between hard and soft dorsal fins; scales on base of dorsal or anal fin

Similar Species: largemouth bass (page 204), shoal bass (page 210), redeye bass (page 208)

Suwannee Bass

mouth extends to center of eye

Largemouth Bass

mouth extends beyond eye

Suwannee Bass

turquoise chin, breast, and belly

Largemouth Bass

Dirty-white chin, breast, and belly

Suwannee Bass

gray-green tail

Redeye/Shoal Bass

red tail

SUWANNEE BASS

Micropterus notius

Other Names: blue belly, river, or riffle bass

Habitat: rocky riffles of medium-to-large rivers

Range: restricted to northern Florida and southern Georgia in the Suwannee and Ochlockonee River drainages

Food: small fish, frogs, insects, crayfish

Reproduction: Spawning takes place when water temperatures reach 60° F; males build nests in the quiet, weedy water along stream edges; males guard the nest and fry.

Average Size: 8–10 in., 1–2 lb.

Fishing Tip: Drift small plastic worms just off the bottom into stream pools.

Notes: Suwannee bass are small bass that rarely exceed 12 inches. They are closely related to redeye and spotted bass. Suwannee bass are river fish and do not naturally occur in lakes. Native to the Suwannee River drainage, they have been introduced into the Aucilla-Wacissa river system in recent years. Though small, they are hard fighters in fast water and prized by fly-fishers who fish for them in small tributaries of the Suwannee River.

Description: back is black to dark olive; silver sides with dark-green or black blotches; back is more arched and the depression above the eye is more pronounced than in the white crappie

Similar Species: white crappie (page 218)

Black Crappie

usually 7–8 spines in dorsal fin

White Crappie

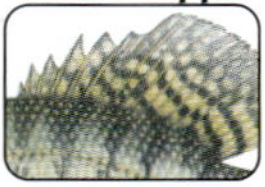

usually 5–6 spines in dorsal fin

Black Crappie

dorsal fin length equal to distance from eye to dorsal

White Crappie

dorsal fin shorter than distance from eye to dorsal

BLACK CRAPPIE

Pomoxis nigromaculatus

Other Names: papermouth, speck, speckled perch

Habitat: quiet, clear water of streams and midsize lakes; often associated with vegetation; roams deep, open basins and flats, particularly during winter

Range: native to central US in Mississippi River basin from Gulf to Great Lakes, historically absent from Atlantic slope drainages north of Virginia; introduced throughout US

Food: small fish, aquatic insects, zooplankton

Reproduction: It spawns in shallow weedbeds from May to June, when water temperatures reach the high 50s; male sweeps out a circular nest, typically on fine gravel or sand; male guards the nest and fry; may spawn in colonies.

Average Size: 6–10 in., 6–16 oz.

Fishing Tip: Try flies under a split shot when the bite is slow.

Notes: Pursued year-round, day and night, crappies are one of North America's most popular panfish. The black crappie is an aggressive carnivore that will hit everything from waxworms and minnows to jigging spoons and small crankbaits. Black crappie actively feeds at night and often suspends itself well off the bottom in pursuit of plankton and baitfish. Requires clearer water and more vegetation than white crappie.

Description: greenish back; silvery-green-to-white sides with 7–9 dark vertical bars; the only sunfish with 5–6 spines in both the dorsal and anal fins

Similar Species: black crappie (page 216)

White Crappie

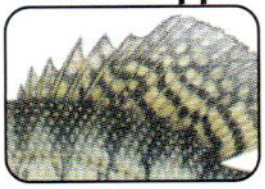

usually 5–6 spines in dorsal fin

Black Crappie

usually 7–8 spines in dorsal fin

White Crappie

dorsal fin shorter than distance from eye to dorsal

Black Crappie

dorsal fin length equal to distance from eye to dorsal

WHITE CRAPPIE

Pomoxis annularis

Other Names: silver, pale, or ringed crappie; papermouth

Habitat: slightly silty streams and midsize-to-large lakes; prefers less vegetation than the black crappie

Range: native to central US, from northeast Mexico to Great Lakes east to Appalachian Mountains; introduced in much of US

Food: aquatic insects, small fish, plankton

Reproduction: It spawns on firm sand or gravel when the water temperature approaches 60° F; male builds a shallow, round nest and guards eggs and young after spawning.

Average Size: 6–9 in., 5–14 oz.

Fishing Tip: In midsummer, slowly troll minnows far behind the boat to locate schools.

Notes: Because black crappies are more tolerant of turbidity and siltation than white crappies, they may be outcompeting white crappies and expanding their range in some areas. Where black and white crappies are found together, they will hybridize. White crappies are often found in large schools suspended off the bottom and away from weeds or structure. They seem to feed more actively at night and under the ice than black crappies.

Description: back and sides dark olive to black, fading to light-olive belly; blue-green spots run in lines down sides; small, dark gill spot; rounded tail

Similar Species: pumpkinseed (page 226), redbreast sunfish (page 228)

Bluespotted Sunfish

small, dark gill spot

Pumpkinseed

red/orange margin on gill spot

Redbreast Sunfish

long, narrow gill flap

Bluespotted Sunfish

short, round pectoral fin

Pumpkinseed

long, pointed pectoral fin

Redbreast Sunfish

short, round pectoral fin

BLUESPOTTED SUNFISH

Enneacanthus gloriosus

Other Names: spotted or bluedot sunfish

Habitat: shallow, weedy lakes and river backwaters

Range: Atlantic coastal plain from southern New York to Florida

Food: aquatic insects, crustaceans

Reproduction: Spawning takes place in May and June, when water temperatures reach the high 60s; male builds a small, round nest in weedbeds and defends the nest and young.

Average Size: 3–4 in.

Fishing Tip: Fish open spots in heavy vegetation.

Notes: There are three species in the genus *Enneacanthus*—the banded, blackbanded, and bluespotted sunfish. All are found along the Atlantic slope, and all are similar in appearance and habits. The bluespotted sunfish is the most common species and can be abundant in the waters of the coastal plain. Bluespotted sunfish are not large enough to be of any value to anglers but are prolific and an important forage fish for larger game fish. They can occupy water with an oxygen content lower than other sunfish require and may be very important in mosquito control in some areas. The breeding males are brightly colored and make great aquarium fish.

Description: dark-green back; dark-olive-to-bluish sides; yellow-to-cream belly; scales flecked with yellow, producing a brassy appearance; dark gill spot with pale margin; large mouth with thick lips

Similar Species: bluegill (page 238)

Green Sunfish

large mouth

Bluegill

small mouth

GREEN SUNFISH

Lepomis cyanellus

Other Names: green perch, bluespotted sunfish, sand bass

Habitat: warm, weedy, shallow lakes and the backwaters of slow-moving streams

Range: native in the Missouri, Mississippi, and Ohio River basins from Appalachians to the Great Plains; widely introduced throughout the US

Food: aquatic insects, crustaceans, small fish

Reproduction: Beginning in May and June, male fans out a nest on gravel bottom near weeds or other cover, often in less than 1 foot of water; male may grunt to lure female into nest; after spawning, male guards nest and fry.

Average Size: 3–8 in., 4–10 oz.

Fishing Tip: At times, green or yellow trout PowerBait is good for green sunfish.

Notes: The green sunfish is abundant in some lakes yet completely absent from others. It is easy to catch but not a popular sport fish because it rarely reaches more than 5 or 6 inches in length. Very tolerant of high siltation and low oxygen levels, it thrives in warm, weedy lakes and backwaters. It often hybridizes with bluegill and pumpkinseed, producing somewhat larger and more voracious offspring.

Description: bluish-green back, fading to orange; about 30 orange or red spots on sides of males; brown spots on females; orange pelvic and anal fins; black gill spot has light margin

Similar Species: bluegill (page 238), green sunfish (page 222), pumpkinseed (page 226)

Orangespotted Sunfish

light margin on gill spot

Bluegill

gill spot lacks light margin

Pumpkinseed

orange or red crescent on gill

Orangespotted Sunfish

hard spines longer than soft rays

Green Sunfish

hard spines shorter than soft rays

ORANGESPOTTED SUNFISH

Lepomis humilis

Other Names: orangespot, dwarf sunfish, pygmy sunfish

Habitat: open to moderately weedy pools in lakes and streams; prefers soft bottoms

Range: Missouri, Mississippi, and Ohio River drainages; Gulf Coast drainages from Texas to Mobile Bay; a few introductions in central US

Food: insects, small crustaceans

Reproduction: Male builds and guards nest in shallow water when water temperatures reach mid 60s; colonial nester.

Average Size: 3–4 in., 3–4 oz.

Fishing Tip: A feisty little fish, it will even bite small, shiny bare hooks.

Notes: This brightly colored sunfish is very common in some lakes, and although it is often caught, it is too small to be a significant panfish. It does, however, make a colorful aquarium pet. The orangespotted sunfish is important as a forage species for other game fish and may be important for mosquito larvae control in some areas. It survives well in silty water and tolerates some pollution, making it well suited for small lakes in agricultural areas.

Description: brown-to-olive back; sides speckled with orange, yellow, blue, and green spots with 7–10 vertical bands; yellow or orange chest and belly; black gill spot has light margin with orange or red crescent

Similar Species: bluegill (page 238), green sunfish (page 222), orangespotted sunfish (page 224)

Pumpkinseed

orange or red crescent on gill flap

Bluegill

gill spot lacks light margin

Orangespotted Sunfish

light margin on gill spot

Pumpkinseed

long, pointed pectoral fin

Green Sunfish

rounded pectoral fin

PUMPKINSEED

Lepomis gibbosus

Other Names: seed, punky, yellow, or round sunfish; bream

Habitat: weedy ponds, clear lakes, slow-moving streams; prefers slightly cooler water than bluegill

Range: native to northern Atlantic slope through Great Lakes to upper Mississippi and Missouri River basins; widely introduced in northern US

Food: insects, snails, fish, leeches, small amounts of vegetation

Reproduction: When water temperatures reach 55° F–63° F; the male builds nest in gravel among weeds in less than 2 feet of water; often nests in colonies with other sunfish species; male aggressively guards the nest; multiple broods per year are common.

Average Size: 5–10 in., 6–10 oz.

Fishing Tip: Waxworms are good pumpkinseed bait, both in summer and winter.

Notes: The pumpkinseed is one of the most beautiful fish in the US. It often schools under submerged logs or deadfalls and around docks. It is easy to catch on small natural and artificial baits and makes fine table fare. Larger specimens often feed along edges of deep weedbeds during the day and settle to the bottom at night. Hybridization with other sunfish is common. In small lakes, pumpkinseeds are known for stunting, filling a lake with a lot of small individuals and only a few larger fish.

Description: dark-olive-green back; olive sides; yellow-orange belly; bright-yellow-orange breast; gill flap long, black, and narrower than the eye; tail slightly forked

Similar Species: bluegill (page 238), green sunfish (page 222)

Redbreast Sunfish

short, round pectoral fin

Bluegill

long, pointed pectoral fin

Redbreast Sunfish

long, narrow, dark gill flap

Green Sunfish

short gill flap with round dark spot

REDBREAST SUNFISH

Lepomis auritus

Other Names: yellowbelly or longear sunfish, sun perch, redbreast bream

Habitat: rocky riffles in streams with medium current; occasionally lakes or reservoirs

Range: Atlantic coastal drainages from southern New York to Florida; introduced in southern Texas

Food: aquatic insects, crustaceans, small fish

Reproduction: It spawns in May and June, when water temperature reaches the high 60s; male builds a small round nest in weedbeds away from the current; male defends nest.

Average Size: 4–8 in., 3–8 oz.

Fishing Tip: Fish small white jigs along rock walls.

Notes: The redbreast sunfish is a small sunfish native to the Atlantic drainage east of the Allegheny Mountains that has been introduced throughout the Southeast. It prefers streams but is frequently found in reservoirs and impoundments. Redbreast sunfish are often found around rocks, logs, or undercut banks near moving water. They are slightly more nocturnal than other sunfish. A popular panfish in many areas, it bites aggressively on small artificial lures and live bait both day and night.

Description: back and sides bronze to dark green, fading to light green; sides have faint vertical bars and small spots; long, pointed pectoral fins; short gill flap with dark spot and red margin in males; yellow or orange breast

Similar Species: bluegill (page 238) and redbreast sunfish (page 228)

Redear Sunfish

red-orange margin on gill spot

Bluegill

round gill spot with clear margin

Redbreast Sunfish

long, narrow, dark gill flap

REDEAR SUNFISH

Lepomis microlophus

Other Names: shellcracker, stumpknocker, yellow bream

Habitat: congregates around stumps and logs in low-to-moderate vegetation in lakes and swamps and large, quiet streams; prefers sand or gravel bottoms; frequents brackish water

Range: native to Atlantic and Gulf slope drainages; lower Mississippi and Ohio River basins; widely introduced in US

Food: mainly mollusks, some small fish and insects

Reproduction: Males build and guard nest in shallow, vegetated water in spring, when water temperatures reach the high 60s; may produce second brood well into summer.

Average Size: 8–10 in., 8–16 oz.

Fishing Tip: Fish with crickets or worms in standing reeds.

Notes: The redear is a large, highly regarded Southern sunfish that has now been introduced in many Northern and Western states. The redear is often found in dense vegetation, where it feeds on snails attached to plant stems. This makes it somewhat harder to locate and catch than other sunfish. The redear is more tolerant of brackish waters than most sunfish and is often found along the deep-water edges of salt marshes and coastal stream mouths.

Description: back is olive-green to black; scales on sides each have a dark-brown spot at base, producing regular rows of spots; lower sides and belly dull red to reddish brown; plain dark gill spot with light margin

Similar Species: bluegill (page 238), redear sunfish (page 230)

Spotted Sunfish

no blotch near rear base of dorsal fin

Bluegill

blotch near rear base of dorsal fin

Spotted Sunfish

rounded pectoral fin

Redear Sunfish

pointed pectoral fin

SPOTTED SUNFISH

Lepomis punctatus

Other Names: stumpknocker, spotted bream, bream

Habitat: slow-moving, weedy streams and rivers with hard bottoms; small ponds

Range: Atlantic slope from North Carolina through Florida; Gulf Coast drainages west to eastern Texas; lower Mississippi River basin

Food: aquatic insects

Reproduction: Males build and guard a solitary nest in shallow, well-vegetated water in spring, when water temperatures reach the high 60s; males guard nest very aggressively.

Average Size: 4–6 in., 2–6 oz.

Fishing Tip: No need to fish for them; they will find you and steal your bait way too often.

Notes: The spotted sunfish is most often found in weedy, slow-moving streams. In many such streams it is the predominant sunfish. Spotted sunfish have a tendency to feed on or near the bottom more than other sunfish. However, spotted sunfish are aggressive feeders, and though often too small to keep, they can be locally very abundant and a persistent bait robber in some streams.

Description: back and sides brown to olive-green; overall bronze appearance; round, pale spots on head and sides; red eye; cheeks scaleless or partly scaled; steeply angled forehead (lower in rock bass); thicker, heavier body than other sunfish; large mouth

Similar Species: green sunfish (page 222), rock bass (page 236), warmouth (page 244)

Roanoke Bass

no scales on cheek

Rock Bass

scales on cheek

Roanoke Bass

no dark margin on anal fin

Rock Bass

dark margin on anal fin

Roanoke Bass

6 spines on anal fin

Green Sunfish

3 spines on anal fin

Warmouth

3 spines on anal fin

ROANOKE BASS

Ambloplites cavifrons

Other Names: rock sunfish

Habitat: warm, small rivers, creeks, and streams with medium current and rocky bottom

Range: native to Tar, Roanoke, Neuse, and Chowan River drainages in Virginia and North Carolina

Food: crayfish, aquatic insects, small fish

Reproduction: It spawns when water temperatures reach the high 60s–70s; males build a small, round nest in shallow water; males guard eggs and fry.

Average Size: 8–10 in., 10–16 oz.

Fishing Tip: Drift small crayfish imitation plastic baits into rocky pools.

Notes: The Roanoke bass is a large sunfish that inhabits only four river drainages, making it one of the most restricted sport fish in North America. It is very similar in appearance to the much more widespread rock bass and was once even considered a subspecies. Unlike rock bass, which are frequently plentiful in lakes, Roanoke bass prefer small, rocky streams. Though they are unknown to most panfish anglers, Roanoke bass have a small-but-ardent following, particularly among fly-fishers.

Description: back and sides brown to olive-green with dark spots and overall bronze appearance; red eye; thicker, heavier body than other sunfish; large mouth

Similar Species: bluegill (page 238), green sunfish (page 222), pumpkinseed (page 226), warmouth (page 244)

Rock Bass

solid dark gill spot

Green Sunfish

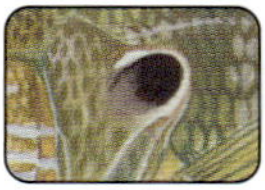

light margin on gill spot

Pumpkinseed

orange or red crescent on gill flap

Warmouth

dark gill spot with light margin

Rock Bass

large mouth extends to eye

Bluegill

small mouth does not extend to eye

ROCK BASS

Ambloplites rupestris

Other Names: redeye, goggle eye, rock sunfish

Habitat: vegetation on firm-to-rocky bottom in clear lakes and medium-size streams

Range: native to upper Mississippi River and Great Lakes basins south through the Tennessee and Mobile Bay drainages; widely introduced

Food: prefers crayfish but eats aquatic insects and small fish

Reproduction: When water temperatures reach the high 60s–70s, the male fans out a coarse gravel nest in weeds and in water less than 3 feet deep; male guards eggs and fry.

Average Size: 6–10 in., 8–16 oz.

Fishing Tip: Fish small dark-green or brown hair jigs on the bottom near weedy rock piles.

Notes: Rock bass are common in clear northern lakes where they frequent weedbeds associated with rocks. Though the rock bass is plentiful, hard-fighting, and good-tasting, it is seldom targeted by anglers, but it is a willing biter and fun to catch on light tackle. The rock bass is often found in schools, which do not stray far from their home territories.

Description: back is dark olive to green, blending to silver-gray, copper, orange, purple, or brown on sides; 5–9 dark vertical bars on sides that fade with age; yellow belly and copper breast; large dark gill spot that extends completely to gill margin; dark spot on rear margin of dorsal fin

Similar Species: green sunfish (page 222) and pumpkinseed (page 226)

Bluegill

small mouth

Green Sunfish

large mouth

Bluegill

dark gill spot

Pumpkinseed

orange crescent

Bluegill

dark spot on dorsal fin

Pumpkinseed

no dark spot

BLUEGILL

Lepomis macrochirus

Other Names: gill, bull, bream, copperbelly

Habitat: medium-to-large streams and most lakes with weedy bays or shorelines

Range: native to central US from Gulf to Great Lakes; absent from Atlantic slope east of the Appalachian Mountains as far south as Virginia; widely introduced in the US, Europe, and South America

Food: insects, small fish, leeches, snails, zooplankton, algae

Reproduction: It spawns from late May to early August; male excavates nest in gravel or coarse sand, in shallow weedbeds often in large colonies of up to 50 nests; often, a smaller "cuckholder" male darts in past the larger guarding male to fertilize the eggs; male guards nest until fry disperse.

Average Size: 6–10 in., 5–10 oz.

Fishing Tip: Adding a kernel of corn to your bait will sometimes entice large bluegills in schools of small ones.

Notes: The bluegill is a favorite of anglers young and old for its tenacious fight and excellent table quality. Small fish are easy to catch near docks in summer. Larger "bulls" favor deep weedbeds close to open water. Bluegills frequently hybridize with other sunfish. All the sunfish have acute daytime vision for feeding on small prey items but see poorly in low light.

Description: back and sides olive-green to silver-green; longitudinal stripes of brown spots on sides; dark, wedge-shaped bar under eye; laterally compressed body; anal and dorsal fins nearly equal in length; dark spot on dorsal fin of young fish; small mouth

Similar Species: green sunfish (page 222), redbreast sunfish (page 228)

Flier

dark bar under eye

Green Sunfish

no bar under eye

Flier

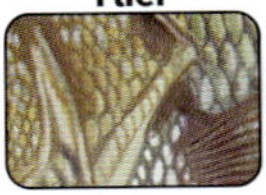

no dark spot on gill

Green Sunfish

dark spot on rounded gill flap

Redbreast Sunfish

long black gill flap

FLIER

Centrarchus macropterus

Other Names: spotfin, silver, round,or swamp sunfish

Habitat: weedy, quiet lakes, creeks, and coastal swamps with a soft bottom

Range: Atlantic coastal plain from Virginia to North Florida; Gulf coastal plain; southern Mississippi River basin

Food: aquatic insects, zooplankton, small fish

Reproduction: It nests in late spring or early summer in dense vegetation; nests are solitary or in small groups; males guard nest and young.

Average Size: 4–6 in., 3–6 oz.

Fishing Tip: Fish with small crickets in thick vegetation.

Notes: Fliers are small sunfish native to the southern Atlantic and Gulf Coasts. This sunfish can withstand lower oxygen levels and higher acidity than most other sunfish. It is very common in still, swampy water. Rarely over 6 inches long, fliers are too small to be an important panfish, but they readily bite and can be proficient bait robbers. When large enough to eat, fliers have flaky, white flesh and fine flavor. Though not a prized panfish, fliers are good predators of mosquito larvae, and small ones should be carefully returned to the water.

Description: blackish back with about 7 dark, irregular vertical bars; large mouth with small teeth around mouth

Similar Species: black crappie (page 216), white crappie (page 218), rock bass (page 236), smallmouth bass (page 206)

Sacramento Perch

12–13 spines in dorsal fin

Black, White Crappie

10 or fewer spines in dorsal

Smallmouth Bass

10 or fewer spines in dorsal

Sacramento Perch

sides have blotchy vertical bars

Rock Bass

spotted sides lack vertical bars

SACRAMENTO PERCH

Archoplites interruptus

Other Names: barred perch; barred, round, or California sunfish

Habitat: weedy lakes, ponds, and slow-flowing streams

Range: native to California's Sacramento–San Joaquin, Pajaro, and Salinas River drainages; introduced in about a dozen Western states

Food: small fish, insects, crustaceans

Reproduction: It matures in 2–3 years; spawns May–August at water temperatures of 71° F–75° F; males establish territories in shallow water; eggs are scattered over algae-covered rocks or plant roots; some researchers have noted egg-guarding behavior by males, while other studies have found no parental care.

Average Size: 6–12 in., 6–16 oz.

Fishing Tip: Troll small spinners very slowly.

Notes: Despite its name, the Sacramento perch is actually a member of the sunfish family and the only native one west of the Rockies. It has a very deep body and so appears rounder than other sunfish. Unlike most other sunfish, Sacramento perch do not build nests but use the nests of other sunfish or natural depressions. They do not school and are not very aggressive, so they are a little harder to catch than other sunfish. Sacramento perch may enter brackish water in coastal areas.

Description: back and sides greenish gray to brown; lightly mottled with faint vertical bands; stout body; large mouth; red eye; 3–5 reddish-brown streaks radiate from eye

Similar Species: bluegill (page 238), green sunfish (page 222), pumpkinseed (page 226)

Warmouth

jaw extends at least to middle of eye

Bluegill

small mouth does not extend to eye

Green Sunfish

jaw does not extend to middle of eye

Warmouth

light margin on gill spot

Pumpkinseed

prominent orange or red crescent on gill spot

Rock Bass

dark gill spot lacks light margin

WARMOUTH

Lepomis gulosus

Other Names: goggle-eye, wide-mouth sunfish, stumpknocker, weed bass

Habitat: heavy weeds in turbid lakes, reservoirs, and slow-moving streams

Range: southern Mississippi and Ohio River drainages to the Great Lakes; southern Atlantic slope drainages from Virginia through Florida; Gulf slope drainage west to the Rio Grande

Food: small fish, insects, snails, crustaceans

Reproduction: Male fans out solitary nest in dense, shallow weeds when the water temperature reaches the low 70s; nest is located by a rock, stump, or weed clump; males guard eggs after spawning.

Average Size: 5–8 in., 6–14 oz.

Fishing Tip: Fish small white or yellow jigs around stumps and logs.

Notes: This secretive sunfish is primarily a lake fish but can be found in the backwaters of large rivers. It is a solitary, aggressive sight-feeder that, when not hiding in dense vegetation, is often found around rocks and submerged stumps. It prefers turbid water and a muddy bottom. It can withstand low oxygen levels, high silt loads, and water temperatures well into the 90s.

Description: bright silver; 6–8 distinct, uninterrupted black stripes on each side; separated dorsal fin has hard spines in front and soft rays in rear; lower jaw protrudes beyond snout

Similar Species: striped bass (page 248), white perch (page 254), wiper (page 250), yellow bass (page 252)

White Bass

single spine on gill cover

Striped Bass

two spines on gill cover

White Bass

horizontal black stripes

White Perch

no stripes except on lateral line

White Bass

single tooth patch on tongue

Striped Bass

two tooth patches on tongue

Striped Bass Hybrid

two tooth patches on tongue

WHITE BASS

Morone chrysops

Other Names: silver bass, streaker, lake bass, sand bass

Habitat: large lakes, rivers, and impoundments with relatively clear water

Range: native to Mississippi and Ohio River valleys to the Great Lakes; Gulf coastal drainages from western Florida to the Rio Grande; introduced in a few large Western lakes

Food: small fish

Reproduction: It spawns in open water over gravel beds or rubble 6–10 feet deep when water temperatures reach 55° F–70° F; a single female may produce more than 500,000 eggs.

Average Size: 8–10 in., 1–2 lb.

Fishing Tip: In the spring, cast imitation-minnow lures into river eddies.

Notes: Common in big rivers, lakes, and impoundments, the white bass is a willing striker and a hard fighter that boasts good table quality. The flesh is dry, and both its flavor and texture can be improved if the fish is quickly put on ice when it's caught. It travels in large schools, frequently near the surface, and can often be spotted by watching for seagulls feeding on frightened baitfish that are fleeing the bass.

Description: dark-gray back; bright-silver sides with 7 or 8 distinct stripes; jaw protrudes beyond snout; separated dorsal fin has hard spines in front and soft rays in rear

Similar Species: white bass (page 246), wiper (page 250), white perch (page 254)

Striped Bass

unbroken horizontal stripes

Wiper

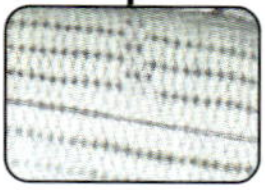

broken horizontal stripes

Striped Bass

two tooth patches on tongue

White Bass

single tooth patch on tongue

STRIPED BASS

Morone saxatilis

Other Names: striper, streaker, surf bass, rockfish

Habitat: coastal marine and estuaries; associated spawning streams; landlocked in some large lakes, reservoirs, and rivers

Range: native to the Atlantic Coast from Maine to northern Florida; Gulf Coast from Florida to the Mississippi River; introduced to inland impoundments and rivers; introduced to Pacific Coast and now present from Baja California to Vancouver Island

Reproduction: Marine fish spawns in freshwater streams; eggs are deposited in riffles at the mouth of large tributaries; eggs must remain suspended to hatch; just a few populations of landlocked fish.

Food: small fish

Average Size: 18–30 in., 10–20 lb.

Fishing Tip: Fish a small jig tied just above a silver spoon.

Notes: Striped bass are a coastal marine fish native to the Atlantic Coast and eastern Gulf. Striped bass are anadromous, living in salt water and migrating into freshwater to spawn. When the Santee and Cooper Rivers were dammed, some striped bass were trapped in the resulting reservoir. These adapted to a freshwater existence and now may spawn in tributary streams. Throughout the US, many introduced inland populations are maintained with hatchery-produced fish. The introduction of the striped bass has created an exciting sport fishery in many large reservoirs. While the marine population of striped bass is declining, the artificially maintained populations are thriving.

Description: dark-gray back; bright-silver sides with 7 or 8 indistinct stripes; separated dorsal fin has hard spines in front and soft rays in rear; two tooth patches, one on back of tongue

Similar Species: striped bass (page 248), white bass (page 246), white perch (page 254)

Wiper

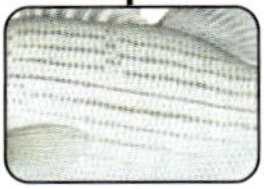

broken stripes

Striped Bass

unbroken stripes

Wiper

2 tooth patches on tongue

White Bass

1 tooth patch on tongue

WIPER

Morone saxatilis x Morone chrysops

Other Names: palmetto, sunshine, or Cherokee bass

Habitat: open water of large lakes and slow-moving rivers

Range: stocked in rivers and lakes in about 40 US states

Food: small fish, insects, crustaceans

Reproduction: This hatchery-produced hybrid is only occasionally fertile.

Average Size: 12–20 in., 3–10 lb.

Fishing Tip: Troll rattle crank baits slowly well behind the boat.

Notes: There are two striped bass hybrids. The sunshine bass is a hatchery cross between a male striped bass and a female white bass. The palmetto bass is the opposite; it is a cross between a male white bass and a female striped bass. Both hybrids are fertile, but there is only limited reproduction. Many states now raise large numbers of these hybrids to stock in waters too warm to support striped bass. This hard-fighting, tasty hybrid has now become a favorite with anglers in areas without good striper populations. The wiper is also becoming an important aquaculture fish, supplying fillets for the grocery store and restaurant market.

Description: sides silvery yellow to brassy; yellowish-white belly; 6 or 7 black stripes broken above anal fin; forked tail; two sections of dorsal fin connected by membrane

Similar Species: white bass (page 246)

Yellow Bass

lower jaw even with snout

White Bass

jaw protrudes beyond snout

Yellow Bass

stripes broken above anal fin

White Bass

stripes continuous

YELLOW BASS

Morone mississippiensis

Other Names: brassy or gold bass; barfish

Habitat: open water over shallow gravel bars in rivers; shallow weedy lakes

Range: Mississippi River drainage from Minnesota to the Gulf; eastern Texas coastal drainages; Mobile Bay drainages

Food: small fish, insects, crustaceans

Reproduction: It spawns in late spring over gravel bars in the mouths of tributary streams.

Average Size: 6–10 in., 8–16 oz.

Fishing Tip: Fish deep backwater sand bars with yellow jigs.

Notes: This close cousin of the white bass is not as common or as popular but is plentiful in many rivers and a few river-bottom lakes. Its schooling and feeding habits are similar to those of white bass, but it tends to stay in the middle of the water column or near the bottom. The yellow bass is a very popular panfish in the southern part of its range, less so in the upper Mississippi River valley; its flaky white flesh is considered by many to be superior to that of white bass.

Description: back is olive to blackish green; silver-green sides with no stripes; front spiny dorsal fin connected by a small membrane to the soft-rayed back portion

Similar Species: yellow bass (page 252), white bass (page 246)

White Perch

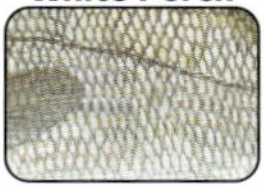

no horizontal stripes except on lateral line

White Bass

black horizontal stripes

Yellow Bass

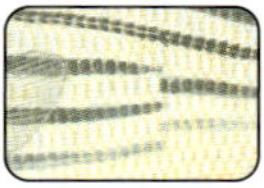

stripes broken above anal fin

WHITE PERCH

Morone americana

Other Names: narrow-mouth bass; silver or sea perch

Habitat: brackish water in coastal areas; nearshore areas of large lakes; expanding range into smaller freshwater lakes and rivers

Range: central Mississippi River and lower Missouri River drainage south to the Gulf; Atlantic Coast from Maine to South Carolina

Food: fish eggs, minnows, insects, crustaceans

Reproduction: Spawning takes place in late spring over gravel bars of tributary streams.

Average Size: 6–8 in., 6–16 oz.

Fishing Tip: Fish white plastic grubs close to the bottom.

Notes: The white perch is primarily a brackish-water fish of the coastal Atlantic states that spawns in tributary streams. There are also a few landlocked freshwater populations in some coastal lakes. The white perch's range is now quickly expanding into many freshwater habitats. They are now common in the Mississippi and Missouri Rivers and the Great Lakes. They prey heavily on fish eggs and are detrimental to native species in many parts of their expanding range. White perch is considered a popular panfish in some areas and as an invasive in others.

Description: olive-green back; yellow-brown sides; many dark bars on sides; slender with pelvic, dorsal, and anal fins well back on body; snout flattened on top; rounded tail; upturned mouth; star-shaped blotch on top of head

Similar Species: brook silverside (page 168) and mosquitofish (page 76)

Lined Topminnow

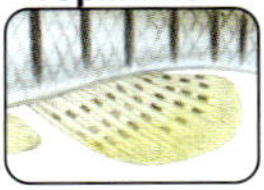

rounded anal fin

Mosquitofish

squared anal fin in females, long and pointed in males

Brook Silverside

long anal fin with straight or concave edge

Lined Topminnow

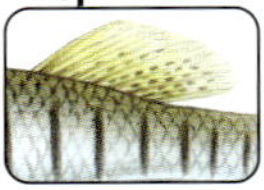

single dorsal fin

Mosquitofish

single dorsal fin

Brook Silverside

two dorsal fins

LINED TOPMINNOW

Fundulus lineolatus

Other Names: lined killifish, barred topminnow, starhead minnow

Habitat: near the surface of stream backwaters, swamps, and pond edges with good vegetation

Range: Atlantic coastal plain from Virginia south to Florida; eastern Gulf coastal plain

Food: insects, crustaceans

Reproduction: From early spring through summer, males defend territories among weeds at stream or pond edges; eggs attach to the vegetation to hatch unattended.

Average Size: 2–3 in.

Fishing Tip: They are a good bait minnow but do not enter minnow traps very well.

Notes: As the name implies, topminnows inhabit the upper water column and are adapted to feeding on or near the surface. The names topminnow and killifish are often interchanged. Though inconspicuous and well camouflaged, they are the favorite target of wading birds. The lined topminnow is common and can be abundant in the coastal plains but is not found in brackish water, as many other topminnow species are. They withstand low oxygen levels well and are often used as bait minnows. Though not very colorful, they make good aquarium fish and readily eat food spread on the water's surface.

Description: back and sides yellow-brown with slight cross-hatching; dark lateral stripe through lips to tail; slender fish with pelvic, dorsal, and anal fins set well back on body; tail, dorsal, and anal fins spotted; long snout flattened on top; rounded tail; upturned mouth

Similar Species: brook silverside (page 168)

Blackstripe Topminnow

front of dorsal behind anal fin origin

Brook Silverside

two dorsal fins

BLACKSTRIPE TOPMINNOW

Fudulus notatus

Other Names: blackstriped killifish, blackbanded topminnow

Habitat: small, slow-moving streams; quiet margins and backwaters of larger streams and rivers; small lakes and ponds

Range: Gulf slope drainage from Mobile Bay to Texas; Mississippi and Ohio River basins to lower Great Lakes

Food: insects

Reproduction: Spawning takes place when water reaches the low 70s; pairs establish territories along stream edges; males aggressively defend territories.

Average Size: 1–2 in.

Fishing Tip: Top minnows are good bait minnows but do not enter traps well so are hard to catch in large numbers.

Notes: Topminnows have an upturned mouth, an adaptation for feeding near the top of the water. In quiet waters, they can often be seen feeding near the surface, where they often turn facing the waves, watching for insects washed their way. Primarily a stream fish that tolerates cloudy water, they are increasingly being seen in small, protected ponds. The names topminnow or killifish are often used interchangeably.

Description: overall silvery, almost transparent appearance; mottled brown, tan, or greenish with dark spots on sides; adipose fin; single dorsal fin with two spines and 10–11 rays

Similar Species: yellow perch (page 120), walleye (page 118)

Trout-Perch

adipose fin

Yellow Perch

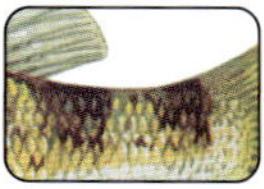

lacks adipose fin

Walleye

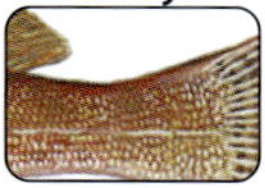

lacks adipose fin

TROUT-PERCH

Percopsis omiscomaycus

Other Names: grounder, sand minnow

Habitat: prefers clear-to-slightly turbid (cloudy) water over sand or gravel; avoids soft-bottomed shallows

Range: central Atlantic slope north through Great Lakes to Mackenzie and Yukon River drainages; Ohio and lower Missouri River basins

Food: insects, copepods, small fish

Reproduction: It spawns May–August over sand bars and rocks in lakes and tributary streams.

Average Size: 3–5 in.

Fishing Tip: A good baitfish, but seining for it is only productive in shallow water at night.

Notes: A deepwater fish by day, the trout-perch is seldom seen unless it washes up on a beach, where it is often mistaken for a juvenile walleye. Nocturnal migration patterns bring large schools into the shallows to feed under the cover of darkness. It is an important forage species for walleyes, northern pike, and lake trout.

GLOSSARY

adipose fin a small, fleshy fin without rays, located on the midline of the fish's back between the dorsal fin and the tail

air bladder a balloonlike organ located in the gut area of a fish, used both to control buoyancy and in the respiration of some species, such as gar; also called the swim bladder or gas bladder

alevin a newly hatched fish that still has its yolk sac

anadromous hatching in freshwater, migrating to the ocean, then reentering streams or rivers from the sea (or large inland body of water) to spawn

anal fin a single fin located on the bottom of the fish near the tail

annulus a mark or ring on the scales, spine, vertebrae, or otoliths, used to determine a fish's age

anterior toward the front of a fish; opposite of posterior

bands horizontal marks running lengthwise along the side of a fish

barbel threadlike sensory structures on a fish's head, often near the mouth; commonly called whiskers; used for taste or smell

bars vertical markings on the side of a fish

benthic organisms living in or on the bottom of a body of water

brood swarm a large group or "cloud" of young fish, such as bullheads

cardiform teeth small teeth on the lips of catfish

carnivore a fish that feeds on other fish (also called a piscivore) or animals

catadromous living in freshwater and migrating to salt water to spawn, such as the American eel

caudal fin the tail or tail fin

caudal peduncle the portion of the fish's body located between the anal fin and the beginning of the tail

cold-water referring to a species or environment; in fish, often a species of trout or salmon found in water that rarely exceeds 70° F; also used to describe a lake or river, according to average summer temperature

copepod a small (less than 2 mm) crustacean that is part of the zooplankton community

crustacean a crayfish, water flea, crab, or other animal belonging to a group of mostly aquatic species that have paired antennae, jointed legs, and an exterior skeleton (exoskeleton); a common food for many fish

dorsal relating to the top of the fish, on or near the back; the opposite of the ventral, or lower, part of the fish

dorsal fin the fin or fins located along the top of a fish's back

eddy a circular water current, often created by an obstruction

exotic species a species not native to a watershed, such as the zebra mussel

fingerling a juvenile fish, generally 1–10 inches in length, in its first year of life

fry a recently hatched young fish that has already absorbed its yolk sac

game fish a species regulated by laws for recreational fishing

gills organs used in aquatic respiration

gill cover the large bone covering the gills; also called the opercle or operculum

gill raker a comblike projection from the gill arch

harvest fish that are caught and kept by sport or commercial fishers

ichthyologist a scientist who studies fish

invertebrates animals without backbones, such as insects, crayfish, leeches, and earthworms

lateral line a series of pored scales along the side of a fish that contains organs used to detect vibrations

length, fork the overall length of a fish from the mouth to the deepest part of the tail notch

length, standard the length of the fish from the mouth to the end of the vertebral column

length, total the length of the fish from the mouth to the tail compressed to its fullest length

mollusk an invertebrate with a smooth, soft body, such as a clam or snail

native an indigenous or naturally occurring species

omnivore a fish or animal that eats plant and animal matter

otolith an L-shaped bone found in the inner ear of a fish

opercle the bone covering the gills; also called the gill cover or operculum

panfish small freshwater game fish that can be fried whole in a pan, such as crappies, perch, and sunfish

pectoral fins paired fins on the sides of the fish, just behind the gills

pelvic fins paired fins below or behind the pectoral fins on the bottom (ventral) portion of the fish

pharyngeal teeth toothlike structures found in the throat on the margins of gill bars

plankton floating or weakly swimming aquatic plants and animals, including larval fish, that drift with the current; often eaten by fish; individual organisms are called plankters

range the geographic region in which a species is found

ray, hard supporting part of the fin; resembles a spine but is jointed (can be raised and lowered) and barbed; found in catfish, carp, and goldfish

ray, soft flexible, sometimes branched structures supporting the fin membrane

scales small, flat plates covering the outer skin of many fish

silt small, easily disturbed bottom particles smaller than sand but larger than clay

siltation the accumulation of soil particles

spawning the process of fish reproduction, in which females lay eggs and males fertilize them

spines stiff, unjointed structures found with soft rays in some fins

spiracle an opening on the posterior portion of the head above and behind the eye

stocking the purposeful introduction of a fish species into an area

swim bladder see **air bladder**

tapetum lucidum a reflective layer of pigment in the eye of walleyes

terminal mouth a type of mouth that faces forward

tributary a stream that feeds into another stream, river, or lake

turbid water water clouded by suspended sediments or plant matter that limits visibility and the passage of light

vent the opening at the end of the digestive tract

ventral the underside of the fish; the opposite of dorsal

vertebrate an animal with a backbone

vomerine teeth teeth found on the roof of the mouth

warm-water a non-salmonid species of fish that lives in water that routinely exceeds 70° F; also used to describe a lake or river, according to average summer temperature

yolk the part of an egg containing food for the developing fish

zooplankton the animal component of plankton; tiny animals that float or swim weakly; common food of fry and small fish

PRIMARY REFERENCES

Bailey, R. M., and W. C. Latta, G. R. Smith. *An Atlas of Michigan Fishes with Keys and Illustrations for Their Identification.* University of Michigan Press: 2004

Becker, G. C. *Fishes of Wisconsin.* University of Wisconsin Press: 1983

Eddy, S., and J. C. Underhill. *Northern Fishes.* University of Minnesota Press: 1974

Hubbs, C. L., and K. F. Lagler. *Fishes of the Great Lakes Region.* University of Michigan Press: 1958

McClane, A. J. *McClane's Field Guide to Freshwater Fishes of North America.* Henry Holt and Company: 1978

Phillips, Gary L., and W. D. Schmid, J. C. Underhill. *Fishes of the Minnesota Region.* University of Minnesota Press: 1982

INDEX

Illustration credits

Cover Illustrations: Bluegill by **Duane Raver/USFWS**

Timothy Knepp/USFWS: 128, 130 (both), 140, 144, 146; **Julie Martinez:** 44, 48, 66 (hickory shad inset), 172 (both), 256; **MyFWC.com/fishing:** 14; **Duane Raver/USFWS:** 13 (both), 25, 26, 28, 30, 32, 34, 36, 38, 40, 52, 54, 56, 58, 60, 62, 66, 76, 82, 94 (bottom), 98 (top), 110, 116 (top), 118, 120, 122, 126, 150 (top), 152, 158, 182, 184, 186, 188 (bottom), 204, 206, 214, 216, 218, 222, 224, 226, 228, 230, 238, 240, 244, 246, 248, 254; **Rawpixel.com/Shutterstock:** 160, 236; **Kate Romenskaya/Shutterstock:** 80, 84, 86; **Joseph Tomelleri:** 46, 64, 68, 70, 72 (both), 78, 92, 94 (top), 98 (bottom), 100 (both), 102, 104, 108, 112 (both), 114, 116 (bottom), 124, 132, 134, 138, 142, 148 (all), 150 (bottom two), 154, 156, 164, 166, 168, 174 (both), 178, 180, 188 (top), 190, 192, 194, 196, 198, 200, 202, 208, 210, 220, 232, 234, 242, 250, 252, 258; **urr_illustration/Shutterstock:** 212

Arctic Grayling (pg. 136) (*Thymallus arcticus arcticus*). A.H. Baldwin (illustrator). From *The Fishes of Alaska,* Evermann, Barton Warren; Goldsborough, Edmund Lee. U.S. Bureau of Fisheries. Washington D.C., 1907.

Fallfish image (pg. 90) from *Third Annual Report of the Commissioners of Fisheries, Game and Forests of the State of New York;* Wynkoop Hallenbeck Crawford, Co. New York and Albany, 1898.

pg. 42 New York Department of Conservation. Ellen Edmondson/Hugh Chrisp, illustrators. *A Biological Survey of the Erie-Niagara System.* Stonecat. Albany, J. B. Lyon Company, 1929.

pg. 42 New York Department of Conservation. Ellen Edmondson/Hugh Chrisp, illustrators. *A Biological Survey of the Upper Hudson Watershed.* Tadpole Madtom. Albany, J. B. Lyon company, printers, 1933.

pg. 50, 74, and 88 from *A biological survey of the Oswego River system.* Albany, J.B. Lyon Company, 1928. Produced for the New York Department of Conservation.

pg. 96from *A biological survey of the Erie-Niagara system.* Albany, J. B. Lyon company, printers, 1929. Produced for the New York Department of Conservation.

pg. 106, 162, 176, and 260 from New York Conservation Department (now Department of Environmental Conservation). Ellen Edmondson and Hugh Chrisp, illustrators.

pg. 170 from *A biological survey of the Champlain watershed.* Albany, J. B. Lyon company, printers, 1930. Produced for the New York Department of Conservation.

ABOUT THE AUTHORS

Dave Bosanko was born in Kansas and studied engineering before following his love of nature to degrees in biology and chemistry from Emporia State University. He spent 30 years as a staff biologist at two of the University of Minnesota's field stations. Though his training was in mammal physiology, Dave worked on a wide range of research projects, from fish, bird, and mammal population studies to experiments with biodiversity and prairie restoration. An avid fisherman and naturalist, he has long enjoyed applying the fruits of his extensive field research to patterning fish location and behavior, and then observing how these fascinating species interact with one another in the underwater web of life.

Dan Johnson is a lifelong angler with a deep fascination for the underwater world. Over the past three decades, Dan has written and edited countless articles on freshwater fish biology, fisheries research, fish behavior, and recreational fishing for magazines including *North American Fisherman* and *In-Fisherman*. He is also a former AdventureKEEN staff editor and the author of *Fish of Colorado* and *Fish of Arizona* field guides. Dan resides in Isanti, Minnesota, with his wife, Julie, and enjoys sharing his love of fish and fishing with friends and family. He counts time on the water with Julie, his children, and grandchildren among life's most precious moments.